Travel Tales

GUY ARNOLD

TRAILBLAZER PUBLICATIONS

Travel Tales
First edition: 2015

Publisher
Trailblazer Publications
The Old Manse, Tower Rd, Hindhead, Surrey, GU26 6SU, UK
www.trailblazer-guides.com

British Library Cataloguing in Publication Data
A catalogue record for this book is available from the British Library

ISBN 978-1-905864-72-0

© **Guy Arnold** 2015

All rights reserved. Other than brief extracts for the purposes of review no part of this publication may be produced in any form without the written consent of the publisher and copyright owner.

Every effort has been made to trace all copyright holders of material quoted in this anthology. If application is made in writing to the publisher, any omissions will be included in future reprints.

GUY ARNOLD describes himself as a freelance. He is the author of more than 40 books. His leading political interest is the Commonwealth; his main area of interest has been Africa and his definitive work published in 2005 was *Africa A Modern History*. His latest book, *America and Britain "Was there ever a special relationship"* was published in 2014. He lived for five years in Canada and became involved in the politics of aid and launched an aid organisation – Canadian Voluntary Commonwealth Service, which subsequently became part of the formal Canadian agency, CUSO. He has lectured for many years on international affairs and his emphasis has been the relationship between North and South. His interest in Africa began in the 1960s when he helped establish the Zambia Youth Service. Thereafter, for a time, he became director of the London-based Africa Bureau. He lives in London.

CONTENTS

INTRODUCTION

1 AFRICA

Zonguldak and Lagos 7
I don't care what they do 9
A Cure for Malaria 11
Nigeria 1975 – a coup 22
Elephant Rocks 25
The Great Pyramid – Giza 26
Baksheesh 28
A Turning Point 30
Camels 31
Locked in the Lavatory 33

2 CANADA

Cap'n Tinkess 40
Wolves 62
Canada by train 63
An autumn lecture tour 66

3 ENGLAND

The Pennine Way 69
A typical day on the Pennine Way 70
Hadrian's Wall 71
A disaster day 73

4 BRITISH GUIANA

The Kaieteur Falls 75
The Melvilles 77
An Amerindian story 79
Another Amerindian story 80
Dadanawa Ranch 80
Maurice Nascimento 84

5 BORNEO

The Plieran River 87
Walking in the Jungle 9

6 SPAIN

The Pilgrim Way 91
The Bible in Spain 92
Lost in Valladolid 94
Carmona 95

7 TURKEY

Jerusalem to Istanbul 97
Dogs 101
I am pleased to meet you 102
Sinop on the Black Sea coast 104
Amasya 106
Erzurum 107

8 EUROPE

Walking through Estonia 109
Indifference and Cheating 110
Politics on the Danube 112
Ouzo (Crete) 114
Tirana to Split 118
Vodka (Rumania) 121
The start to a long walk 122

9 ASIA/EUROPE

Breakfast in Amman 125
Georgia: seeking accommodation 127
The military road to Russia and Qazbegi 129
Into Iran 133

10 A MISCELLANY

Glencoe: the North Face 135
White Bermuda 137
Albuquerque 139

INTRODUCTION

I have always believed that the best way to get to know a country is by foot – walking. Those who travel by car miss so much. In their determination to reach the next monument they miss the little things that enrich any journey.

This is not an orthodox travel book with a beginning and end. Rather, from a life in which I have done much travelling I have selected scenes and encounters that were different or had special significance, at least for me. The time span of these anecdotes stretches from 1951 when I thought I could tackle the forbidding North Face of the Buchaille Etive Mor at the head of Glencoe to 2012 when finally I tackled the Pennine Way. Sometimes, I travelled by train or bus, depending upon the distance between two stopping places and often I was drawn to a place – Amasya in Turkey – for its longevity as a city and the scenic beauty of its situation. Three entries – *Cap'n Tinkess*, *A Cure for Malaria* and *Locked in the Lavatory* – are written as short stories. I have had four travel books published and have drawn from them for stories or incidents. These are *Longhouse and Jungle* (Borneo), *Down the Danube*, *Journey Round Turkey* and *In the Footsteps of George Borrow*. I have divided the stories according to place under the following headings: Africa, Canada, England, British Guiana (then still a British colony), Borneo, Spain, Turkey, Europe, Asia (Europe), a Miscellany. I have done other long walks for example – in Crete or the Black Forest. In 1964 with a co-driver in a long wheel-base Landrover we journeyed from Lusaka in Central Africa to Dar es Salaam and then Mombasa where we took ship in "The State of Bombay" to India – the journey took nine days, long enough for an Indian fellow passenger to teach me bridge. Across India to Calcutta and then to pioneer what became the "hippie trail" back to England, which took in Pakistan, Afghanistan, Iran, Iraq, Jordan, Syria, Lebanon, Turkey, Greece, Yugoslavia (as it was then), Italy and France.

I am not a Rambler because I like my walks to be solitary for solitude encourages thinking. Three of my last entries are set in England: the Pennine way that I had repeatedly set aside because it was always there to be walked later; and Hadrian's Wall, which the Victorian artist romanticised by painting a solitary Roman soldier standing guard against the Picts and Scots. Walking in Spain over three months I developed a routine: I would begin my day's walk between seven and eight o'clock after a good breakfast and walk up to 35 (and sometimes 40) kilometres until reaching my destination – a village or town where I could find accommodation. I would then have a late midday meal before settling into my room. Then I would spend two hours more or less examining the town and any outstanding features, return to my room for a rest and then sally forth to find the best eating place for my supper – the highlight of a long day.

Guy Arnold, January 2015

AFRICA

Zonguldak and Lagos

Humanity versus officialdom. In 2001 I went from Istanbul along the Black Sea coast of Turkey into Georgia. Zonguldak, a small town near the beginning of my journey, was beautifully sited and my hotel was perched on a cliff top 300 feet above a startlingly blue sea that was almost vertically beneath me when I sat on my veranda. Just off shore was a small island occupied by a lighthouse. After travel in Georgia I returned to Turkey. In Erzurum I tried to identify the hills that are meticulously described by John Buchan in Greenmantle. My journey then took me to Diyarbakir and through a region that was a no go area for strangers as it was involved in the Kurdish insurrection against the Turkish government. I planned an overnight stay in the bustling modern city of Kharamanmaras. I booked into a hotel and deposited my passport with the receptionist as was normal practice. In my room I part unpacked my rucksack and was preparing to have a shower when there was a knock on my door: it was the receptionist, apologetic but

"These two gentlemen would like to talk with you."

They were plainclothes policemen. One was the silent one, the other set about questioning me: where had I been, why was I in Turkey, what did I propose to do next? As he expanded his catalogue of questions my travel diary – a fullscap sized notebook with rings that allowed pages to be detached – which was obtruding from my rucksack caught his eye:

"What is this" he asked, his voice registering rising suspicion, so I extracted it and handed it to him. By pure chance the name Zonguldak in capital letters was at the top of the page ready to be examined.

"Zonguldak?" he said, "I was born in Zonguldak" and then, clearly motivated by happy childhood memories he handed the notebook back to me shook hands and wished me a happy time in his country.

I was in Nigeria at the time of the coup which replaced Gowon as military head of state with Murtala Mohamed. I had in any case been on the point of returning to England for family reasons. The airport, I found, was bristling with soldiers and they had replaced the airport staff that normally examined luggage. As far as I could see all the soldiers were young and hovering on the edge of being aggressive. I put my case on the long examination table opposite a soldier who was still in his teens and held his rifle as though about to start shooting.

"Open up" he said brusquely. I did so. By chance the last thing I had packed was a leather-bound book-shaped display folder for photographs. Money was what the soldiers had been instructed to look for and my soldier focused suspiciously upon the folder. "What's this?" he demanded so I opened the folder to reveal a full length colour photograph of a Yoruba chief in ceremonial regalia. The young soldier's expression changed from aggressive suspicion to friendly interest.

"Is this your friend?" he asked.

"Yes."

He looked again at the photograph, closed the folder and placed it back on my clothes, shut and locked my case and put a large chalk mark on it and smiled me through.

Turkey and Nigeria

I don't care what they do

Like the fabled Roman roads this one ran dead straight over mile upon mile of the red earth as my landrover created a dust cloud to mark our passing. I had come 150 miles and had more than 100 still to go. Then I swore. Steam was rising from under the bonnet. I drew into the side, got out and lifted the bonnet. The fan belt had gone and I had no spare. I could hear the bubbling of the water. Only then did I take account of my surroundings. I was in open bush country, bleak and uninviting that stretched endlessly on either side of the road.

As luck would have it I had stopped by a farm gate and barbed wire stretched on either side of it. Two hundred yards from the gate was a lonely bungalow but there was no sign of life either human or animal. I opened the gate and was careful to close it behind me before walking to the drab, uncared for dwelling that had not seen a coat of paint in years. A low veranda ran the length of the bungalow. I stepped up onto it and was about to call out when a woman appeared. She was anything between forty and sixty and had hardened with work that, I guessed, had never brought in much reward. She had a long, wrinkled neck like a chicken and a careworn face, lined and bleak like the countryside. But the most noticeable thing about her were her hands: they were disproportionately large in relation to her tall, thin body, work worn and capable like those of a labouring man they represented the life she had lived in this lonely outpost of Afrikanerdom. Her brown hair was losing the battle as grey advanced in streaks; it was drawn back in an untidy bun. She looked me over for a moment.

"Yes" she said without expression.

"I wonder if you can help. My fan belt has broken and I have no spare." Surprise at my English accent had registered momentarily as something unexpected, then,

"Wait here" she said and disappeared into the bungalow. Five minutes must have passed before she reappeared with a huge spanner and fan belt in one hand and a full watering can in the other. I took the watering can from her and in silence we walked up the drive, opened and closed the gate behind us and approached my still steaming landrover,

"I don't suppose you know how to mend it", she said.

"No" I said.

"I didn't think so", she said.

Using her huge man-like hands she fixed her fan belt in my vehicle in two minutes, tightened the screws with her huge spanner and then, "We must feed the water in carefully", which we did until the watering can was empty. She lowered the bonnet.

"You had better come up to the house" she said and side-by-side we walked the two hundred yards to her bungalow. On the veranda she said, "Wait here" and disappeared. Repairs were needed, the house was falling apart and I guessed she had no permanent help. There had not been even a dog to bark at me. Then she reappeared carrying a large round tray on which reposed two big tumblers and an unopened bottle of Black Label Whisky. She placed the tray on a low wicker table that occupied the centre of the veranda. There were two wicker chairs, one on either side of it, and in silence we sat in them. The silence was an agreed silence. She clearly had no small talk and I could think of nothing to say that would be appropriate to our present circumstances. She opened the inviting bottle of Black Label and poured a triple measure into each large tumbler – there was no accompanying soda or water or ice. When we had finished our whiskies – in unison as it were – she poured a second equally large measure for each of us. These we drank again in silence. I like my whisky but I still had a long drive ahead of me. Then she spoke:

"I am going to stay here – I don't care what they do." She stared across her land to the wire fence and beyond into the endless bush and an unfathomable future.

I rose and thanked her for her help – she gave the slightest inclination of her head as an acknowledgement. I walked down the drive, carefully shut the gate and looked back. She stood as I had left her, staring into the distance. I got into my landrover and drove away.

Central Africa 1965

A Cure for Malaria

I never tired of driving into the African dawn whose suddenness across the landscape brought everything to dramatic light at breath taking speed. I had been driving for most of the night and had stopped to stretch my legs at the roadside with the sun still out of sight behind a ridge of trees and three giraffes, tall silhouettes, gracefully loped from one side of the road to the other a hundred yards ahead.

I had turned off the main road as directed and soon came to the house. It should have been set in the soft rural Midlands of England surrounded by elm trees with rooks cawing in the upper branches. Instead it rose majestic and mellow in its weathered yellow sandstone here in the middle of the African bush. It was two stories high and a splendid balcony ran half the length of the house above the heavy studded front doors.

I stopped on the gravel and descended stiffly from my landrover; I had clocked 501 miles almost non-stop. The gravel formed a semi-circle in front of the house and then, beyond a deep green hedge a formal garden stretched for the best part of 100 yards to a line of great evergreens, tall, shaped like poplars, a row of sentinels to provide a wall to protect the houses' facade. Beyond them, just a glimpse through the trees was the lake whose waters shimmered in the heat. It was midday.

The Colonel stood in the great doorway, upright, not depending upon the walking stick in his right hand but carrying it as a necessary adjunct, a weapon in case of need. A big, solid, thick figure whose strength had not been diminished by old age, in his prime he must have been a man of immense physical vitality. He was bald now, except for a trimming of hair round the sides and back of his great head whose close-cropped whiteness emphasised the head's bullet quality. His eyes, blue and deep, had lost nothing with age of their penetrating sharpness but his face was dominated by the great hook nose. Hacking his empire out of this bush nearly half a century before he would have done the work of four men himself while driving everyone else to do double.

Now he had mellowed like his house and his recreation was to entertain those who passed through this remote corner of the land and he did so on a princely scale. He greeted me warmly for it was not my first visit. He enquired as to my drive and chuckled when he heard it had been through the night and non-stop.

"Water has been taken to your room", he told me as he turned to lead the way. His pace was the shuffle of an old man despite the bull frame. We passed through the gloomy, stone-flagged hall and into the cloisters. The house had been built in a square round an inner garden and cloisters ran round its four sides.

"I have put you in the Venetian room" he said as we halted by a door on the third side of his cloisters. "Come up as soon as you are ready, I expect you feel like a drink."

My room had great coloured Venetian prints, several seventeenth century busts, and a massive oak bed. I went through the cloisters, and across the stone-flagged hall and up to the veranda where the Colonel waited for me. The Colonel came from a distinguished family and when he built the house he had done so with the pride of anticipation and certainty as though he would be here forever. He had recreated for himself in this remote African bush a corner of an old and vanishing England. He had managed this both with the architecture and then with the treasures of family furniture from his estate; these he had brought out over the years on his return from trips he made back to England.

The Colonel's personal manservant Paul waited upon us. He provided me with a gin and tonic while I stood on the balcony listening to the Colonel telling me a story about the lake – his lake. Later Paul reappeared, discrete yet familiar with the possessiveness of a trusted retainer whose presence went without saying. He was almost as old as the Colonel and had been with him for 40 years. They would both have been lost without each other. Lunch was ready.

It was a Saturday and I was to stay overnight. Then I could travel to my destination in more leisurely style on the Sunday.

The Colonel, I knew, wanted me to attend his little church for the weekly service in the morning. We would rest until three-thirty when the Colonel would call for me to go to his hot springs for a picnic. It was an honour to be taken to his hot springs. In my bedroom I sat on the side of the bed conscious of a tugging, throbbing ache in the region of the kidneys. I arched my back and pressed my hands into the ache; it must have been the result of the long drive, the constant jolting of the landrover over endless miles of dirt road.

I was aware of the knocking on the door for some time before I responded. I was lying on my back on the bed, my feet over the side. I struggled into a sitting position and looked at my watch. It was half past three and the Colonel was outside calling me to tea at his hot springs; I called back that I was coming. I must have blacked out for the last thing I remembered was sitting on the bed feeling the pain in my back. I brushed my hair, shook my head and went to the door. There stood the Colonel, stick in hand, solid, courteous, ready for his pleasure: he wanted to show me his hot springs and enjoy my enjoyment of them.

"You had a good sleep?" he enquired. I wondered how many times he had knocked to wake me.

"Yes indeed" I said and fell in beside him, adjusting to his pace. Slowly, an old man's shuffle, he started along the cloisters, talking as he went but concentrating all the time upon what he was doing, looking straight ahead to make sure of his steps. He described how he had discovered the hot springs all those years ago.

I was lying on my back staring up at a strange ceiling with blue sky off to the left. For a moment I tried to figure out where I was but then I saw the cloisters and on my other side the door to the Venetian room. There was no sign of the Colonel. I scrambled to my feet, conscious of the pain in the back of my head. I must have fallen straight back and cracked it on the stone paving. How extraordinary for me to black out like that, I thought but then the recollection of my sleep that afternoon made me realise that it was the second time. I hurried into the dim hall. Halfway across it, heading for the bright sunlight framed in the open front door, the Colonel was moving at his slow shuffle, still talking about the discovery of his hot springs. He had not noticed my temporary absence. I fell in beside him.

Outside on the gravel the Colonel turned to me: "Paul is bringing the picnic basket, then we can ….."

I was staring up at the brilliant blue sky above me, once more spread-eagled on my back. The Colonel looked down in amazement.

"Are you all right?" he began.

I scrambled to my feet, ashamed of such an astonishing display of weakness.

"I don't usually faint, it is most odd", I said.

"You are all right, then?"

"Yes of course, it must have been a spell of dizziness."

We walked slowly across the gravel to the hedge that separated the gravel from the landscaped garden below.

"Most odd" I repeated as I clutched handfuls of the hedge in a vain effort to control my next collapse. Once more I stared up at the sky.

"Are you sure you are all right?" The Colonel's voice had risen a decibel, there was the slightest edge to it although good manners prevented him from suggesting that I was behaving in an unusual fashion. I got to my feet somewhat more slowly than the previous time, shook my head, nodded as though in confirmation that all was well.

"Are you sure you feel up to coming out to my hot springs then, we don't have to go you know."

"Certainly" I replied, "I am looking forward…." This time as I lay on my back the blue of the sky was obscured as the Colonel bent over me, the great beak of his nose like a bird of prey approaching my eyes.

"I think something is wrong with you" he said. Once more I scrambled, but in slow motion to my feet. The Colonel, meanwhile, had turned towards the house and was calling, his stentorian voice as strong as it must have been on the battlefield of his estate over the years: "Paul, Henry, come at once."

"I am sure it is just a passing phase", I said as I began to weave unsteadily towards the door. I didn't make it. Yet again

I stared up at the blue heavens and wondered why I didn't simply stay down. But the Colonel's calls had brought the two old servants from the house and the indignity of lying there impelled me to my feet once more unaided.

"I think we had better get you to bed" the Colonel said and unprotesting now I walked slowly towards the door, Paul hovering at my side, Henry receiving instructions from the Colonel – I only distinguished the word "doctor". Then we were inside the gloomy hall and with quick guile, to evade Paul's available assistance, I managed yet another spectacular collapse, spread eagling myself once more flat on my back on the cold flagstones of the hall. I heard, as though it was a distant and unconnected event, the crack as the back of my head made contact with the stone. I was conscious of the Colonel, now showing distinct signs of agitation, standing in the doorway and blocking out most of the light while Paul knelt beside me wondering what to do.

Paul helped me to my feet, the Colonel giving directions, and slowly now we passed through into the cloisters. In the Venetian room I collapsed onto the bed while Paul and Henry who had materialised again undressed me. A period of booming and looming followed: great sounds as though made at the other end of a vast tunnel-like hall came echoing towards me. When they arrived they passed straight through my forehead and out the other side, exiting from the back, which had become a permanent throbbing ache. And then, following the noises, came the shapes: huge indeterminate masses reared up and loomed over me, dark, menacing shiny black clouds that turned into giant withered prunes before they joined together to form fire-like arrows which shot into my head while I tossed desperately from side to side in a hopeless effort to avoid them. My sheets were soaked with sweat. My lips felt enormous, my body so heavy that I could only move one small part of it at a time in an unresponding slow-motion as I concentrated all my attention upon it. Then a moment of terrible silence would follow before the sounds boomed once more from the end of the tunnel and the cycle began all over again.

Later, there were people round the bed. The Colonel was there; I could hear his voice quite distinct and clear, penetrating the other confusions: "Here is the dresser from the clinic – my doctor", he said while an elderly African took my finger and pricked it for a blood sample. Then they gave me medicine and went away and instantly, even before they had left the room, the booming started again.

The Colonel had returned with Paul hovering in the background in support.

"Malaria of course" he said "you are full of it, the doctor tells me he has never seen so much of it in the blood." Even in my disoriented condition I could distinguish the satisfaction with which he said this as though my malaria represented another first in a lifetime of collecting.

"I have just the medicine for you" he went on, "can you manage to sit up?" I only wanted to lie in my soaking sheets and be boomed at but there was a compulsion about the old Colonel – it was what had ensured the eventual success of his estate – and not wanting to disappoint my host I heaved myself onto one elbow, my head spinning, sweat dripping down my face. At the same time I saw quite clearly: Paul was holding a tray and on it stood a single glass half full of red wine. "Claret" said the Colonel. I took the glass with a shaking hand and gulped at the wine. Deftly Paul retrieved the glass before I collapsed back ready for the looming shapes. These arrived at once and took all my attention even though, somewhere in the back of my mind, I was conscious of the Colonel and his servant leaving the room.

Perhaps an hour later, for daylight still showed through the window, I came out of my nightmare, limp but temporarily lucid, as the door opened and the Colonel came once more to my bedside followed again by Paul holding a tray.

"I don't suppose you feel like food?" he asked and then, at the sight of my blank face, answered his own question:

"No, of course not. What you need is more medicine." He stood aside and Paul moved forward with his tray.

"Sherry" said the Colonel and I grasped a heavy, beautiful crystal glass and with two gulps swallowed this second dose of medicine. I downed it quickly because I could feel the tunnel approaching me again and I had to return into a position to receive the attacking noises and shapes. Only flat on my back could I deal with them; that way they could come in the front of my forehead and out the back through the throbbing pain where a lump had now formed and into the soaked pillow. So I collapsed back onto my wet sheets. The Colonel retreated in good order, followed by Paul and the booming and looming began all over again.

Periodically I escaped from the tunnel to lie in soaked exhaustion waiting fearful, like a child that has waked from a nightmare, trying to grasp at quiet and peace before I felt myself slipping once more and knew I was returning to the tunnel. When this happened I would attempt, feebly, to stay in the world I knew but to no avail. I would hear, disembodied, as though it were not a part of me, a strangled moan escape my lips and then, once more, I would be in my tunnel waiting in terror for the roaring sounds to rush through me before the shapes arrived. How long this went on I do not know but when the next period of lucidity returned it was dark. I lay for a while enveloped in the silence of the old house except for the distant but steady hum of the generator somewhere in the background. And then the door opened and the light, a dim one, was snapped on. The now familiar procession arrived: the Colonel with Paul in attendance holding a tray.

"Have you ever tried white port? It is an excellent drink. I have put a lump of ice in it." Slowly I moved the leaden weights of my body into a half sitting position to prop myself on an elbow while Paul lowered the tray for me to take the glass. That was the best white port I have ever drunk. I sank back at once, exhausted by the effort, ready for the coming horrors and shakes.

The Colonel was speaking again, far off now: I shall come in an hour with your night medicine before we turn off the generator." I think I nodded from my prone position, at least I tried to do something which sent an agony of protest through the back of my head. The Colonel left the light on

18 A CURE FOR MALARIA

though I was only half aware of it when I surfaced briefly between my booming tunnels and looming shapes. The effect they had upon me was one of total drainage: I felt as though all the sap, the blood, everything had simply been drained from my body to leave me limp and empty and light for there was nothing inside me although I could only move with the greatest effort. This irritated me; I ought to be able to move my featherweight body with ease but the opposite was the case. Arguing fiercely with myself about this apparent irrationality I was drawn back into my tunnel once more.

I don't know what time it was when the Colonel returned – probably an exact hour had passed, he was punctilious in these matters – for he turned the generator off early.

"More pills" he announced when he saw I was lying open-eyed "and a brandy. That should do the trick", he added with satisfaction. This time Paul had two glasses on his tray: a large tumbler of water and an elegant brandy snifter, Georgian by the look of it, with a generous portion of golden brown liquid filling the lower third of it. There were three pills, which I swallowed with the water. Then, gratefully, I grasped the snifter and drank the brandy in a long slow steady gulp. Medicine! The Colonel stood watching me with approval.

"We'll have you right by tomorrow" he said in the tones of a man who relied upon experience rather than a doctor's prescriptions. "The generator goes off in five minutes. Good night to you." And he shuffled to the door followed by the faithful Paul with the tray of empty glasses.

That night was endless. At first, after the Colonel had left, I lay still in the lighted room, wondering without much hope whether the worst of the fever was past. Then the light dimmed and flickered out as the noise of the generator died away somewhere in the distance. The house became silent. I lay in the dark like a child trying not to be frightened, waiting for the nightmares to begin again. But nothing happened and tentatively, defying fate, I turned slowly onto my side. I must have dropped off but I do not remember. Then the booming began again, starting from an immense distance as though it might not find me but then, just as I thought it was aiming at some other hapless soul in another place, it closed in upon me with a final terrible rushing sound that made my head explode. The shapes followed, weird and different, the predominant colour now brown-yellow. I fought for endless hours: the booming, the shapes, the fire arrows piercing their ways into my head. And between them came silences that were so terrible I wanted the shapes to return. I tried to move but was weighted down like lead. I lay in a lake of my own sweat and shivered and burned alternately and sometimes, it seemed did both together. Once I tried to go to the bathroom but collapsed onto the cold stone floor instead and in a frantic desperation dragged myself back onto the bed and pulled the sheets and blanket round my chin to await the coming of the shapes again. In the end sheer exhaustion allowed me to sleep. I awoke, limp but lucid. The fever abated as grey light through the window brightened quickly to announce the new dawn.

The knock on the door awoke me but from a normal sleep. In came the Colonel and this time Paul was bearing a cup of tea on his tray.

"Ah, I see you are awake. How do you feel?"

"Weak, but the fever has gone." I managed a grin.

"You must stay in bed this morning and rest up." It was a statement but a statement containing the hint of a question and I knew at once how to reply. In many respects the old Colonel was like a child. Tough and ruthless, he had spent a lifetime getting his own way and wearing out those around him in the process, including his own family. Now in his old age he took an almost childlike pleasure in displaying the fruits of his long life of struggle for others to admire.

"But I must come to the morning service in your church" I replied and though he managed to control most of his expressions I could see he was moved as his fierce old eyes glinted with pleasure. "You think you can make it?"

I tried to nod from my pillow but that was a mistake for it hurt the back of my head. "Yes, as long as I take things slowly. What time is it now?"

It was just past six and the service was at eight.

"You continue to rest; I'll send Henry at seven with some hot water for shaving. Then you can take your time getting up. We will have breakfast after the service." I fell asleep at once when he left to be woken by Henry an hour later. It took me the whole of that hour to shave and dress. There was a chair in the bathroom and after two strokes with the razor I would sit back in it, my head swimming, grasping the front of the basin to steady myself before struggling to my feet again to tackle another slice of lather. My hand trembled with the effort and I was afraid of cutting myself.

I dressed just as slowly, one piece of clothing at a time, but I was ready when at ten to eight the Colonel came to take me to church. Reduced by my own weakness I had no need to adjust my pace to the Colonel's old man's shuffle, it was all I could manage through the cloisters and dim hall onto the gravel and then round the side of the house to the little chapel. The chapel was of a piece with the house. When we came round the corner the Colonel stopped to explain its history. The pause was none too soon. He had built it for the sake of his workers,

"They are a religious people" he explained and the service was conducted entirely in the local dialect. At that moment the African lay preacher came to us, shook hands respectfully with the Colonel who then introduced him to me. Other Africans, standing in groups outside the little chapel turned and greeted us with traditional claps and inclinations of the body. Nothing could have been more feudal.

"You do not need to stand up during the service", the Colonel told me. He explained this to the preacher and then led me inside.

There was some fine carving in that chapel which he pointed out to me as we moved slowly up the little aisle. He placed me in the tiny choir to the side while he took up his own place in the great carved single seat reserved for him. The chapel was full and the service long, all in the local dialect, and my head swam again as they stood up to sing psalms and hymns and knelt to pray and stood to sing again, and then sat for a long sermon. I have no religion but had come because I knew my presence would give pleasure to my host. The Colonel was not religious either but the chapel and the sermons and his presence were part of the world he had created for himself. His was an entirely squirearchical religion, that which was expected of him by his people – he always referred to them as his people – and absolutely right, part of the world he had created for himself. The Africans accorded him his place as the head of their community without question and he responded in kind. I doubt the old man had ever had a religious thought in his head.

When that interminable service finally ended we filed out onto the gravel and stood for ten minutes while most of the congregation lined up to greet the Colonel and me. Eventually we returned to the house.

We had breakfast together. I was pleased to find that my appetite was returning, and then at the Colonel's suggestion I retired to my room for a rest. I would set off at eleven – Paul was to provide sandwiches and the Colonel insisted that Henry came with me in the landrover "just in case you collapse at the wheel" he said. Just what Henry would do in such circumstances except be thrown into a ditch with me I could not imagine, for he did not drive himself. But the Colonel was adamant.

"He can return by the bus tomorrow morning" he said, "he has relatives there."

Henry came to my room at eleven and took my bag. I walked through the cloisters looking at a scene whose oncoming decay would set in the moment the Colonel died and out through the dim stone-flagged hall onto the gravel where my landrover stood, its metal already burning to the touch in the baking sun. The Colonel waited to see me off. We shook hands, I climbed in and started the engine, Henry placed my bag at the back and then got in at the other side, the Colonel nodded and I was off again, back to the endless dirt roads and ridges, my bout of malaria cured, already only an incident, an inconvenience disposed of in the great house by means of claret and sherry and white port and brandy. It would not have been right to overstay my welcome and I had work to do.

Zambia 1965

Nigeria 1975 – a coup

I spent two months in the summer of 1975 researching for a book I had been commissioned to write about Nigeria. I had the use of a flat in Ikedja, which was a part of greater Lagos. It was July when the temperature averaged 80 degrees plus and at least one heavy fall of rain could be expected every day, usually mid-afternoon.

On this particular occasion, late in July, I spent the day writing in the flat. I sat by a window that overlooked the street and from time to time broke off my writing to watch the preparations for a funeral that were taking place in the street below.

The funeral was for a very old man who lived in the house next door. He was reputed to be in his mid-nineties. Many relatives and friends had been coming and going all day for the wake but the time had come for the burial. A big marquee had been erected outside the house in which trestle tables and benches had been arranged for the feast that would come later that afternoon. A heavy downpour of rain had left steaming puddles the length of the dirt road. A huge hearse had the ornate coffin loaded into it and then along either side sat, squashed together, women and children.

At last it was deemed to be ready to go and the driver solemnly came from the front and shut the rear door, testing the handle several times to make sure it was firmly closed. A semi-circle of women stood at the rear of the hearse to watch its departure. Other watchers stood outside the marquee. The driver got into the front seat behind the wheel then with a roar the hearse lurched forward two yards and then stalled. The back door flew open, and a small child was catapulted out onto the road and began bawling. The circle of women raised their hands and said "OH" in unison, one ran forward and picked up the child, which was returned to the hearse. The driver came round, as solemn as before, closed the back door of the hearse, tested it and then went back to drive. Another lurch and the same child was ejected from the hearse onto the road and this time one of the women picked it up and carried it bawling into the marquee. Shaking his head in disbelief the driver went back a third time and started the hearse which this time went smoothly on its way to the claps and cheers of the watching crowd. Later the tables were all rearranged along the street, a crowd gathered as apparently endless dishes of food were produced, a band played and the wake continued into the small hours.

When General Gowon arrived in Uganda for the annual OAU meeting at the end of July 1975, he was greeted with all the honours and special attention due to the leader of Africa's largest and most influential state. Two days later, as he sat in the hall with all the other heads of state an aide came to whisper in his ear. He quietly left the hall. In Nigeria he had been replaced by Murtala Mohamed as head of state and his nine years rule had come to an end. The coup, which was bloodless, had come and gone very quietly; more like the change of managing director than anything else.

Over the radio at seven in the morning a Colonel announced that the military had changed the government; everyone was told to keep calm; essential workers had to go to their jobs but everyone else had a "work free day". This message was repeated over the radio every half hour for the next twelve hours and between each repeat martial music was played. At one point the martial music record got stuck – it was a recording of the Band of the Royal Marines – and whoever was managing the studio had forgotten how the record ended for he lifted the arm up and placed it near the end of the record and we were treated to a rendering of "God Save the Queen". Red faces! The new head of state broadcast at seven that evening but he didn't outline any programme of action.

The following day everyone went back to work although a curfew had been imposed and everyone had to be at home by seven. This was impossible. Lagos stands near the top of world rankings for traffic jams and many people sit for three ours in their cars at the end of the day before they can reach their homes. As a result of the curfew all offices and shops shut at three to give people time to get home before the curfew came into operation. The result was greater chaos than ever and the curfew was lifted the next day. Back to normal!

However, the country's borders were closed and telephone connections with London had been closed, posing severe problems for journalists. I entrusted several articles to a business friend who was able to leave but later I learned they had been seized by customs. I set off on a ten-day trip round the north of the country, which I had planned before the coup.

A number of western journalists, mainly British, had tried to get into Nigeria but had been turned back at the borders. They then hired a private plane and flew into northern Nigeria where they dispersed in search of news. The new government denounced this behaviour and the military set up road blocks in the north of the country.

By then I was staying with a friend in Kano and one afternoon we went on a visit outside the city. We ran into a military roadblock and the soldiers demanded my passport. I had left it in my briefcase back at my host's house. The military insisted I stayed by the road block while my host went back to get my briefcase and returned with it an hour later. The officer in charge flipped through it and then told me to come to a barracks in Kano the next morning at nine o'clock.

I was on time and they were waiting for me. I was shown into a small room devoid of any furniture except for an upright desk and chair fixed to the floor. I was invited to sit at the desk. One officer stood directly behind me, the other in front. He told me he had been through my passport and I had not been stamped into the country. I told him the date of my arrival in June and he flipped through my passport again but could find no stamp. I asked him for it and began my own search. As it happened my passport was full and ready to be changed and after going through it twice while the officer looked at me with deepening suspicion and the man behind me maintained an ominous silence, I remembered my entry into the country. The customs officer had complained that my passport was full and there was no empty space. In the end he had turned to the middle and stamped my entry across a small space between two pages with very faint ink. I now turned to the centre of my passport, just managed to identify the stamp, explained what had happened on my entry and passed it to my interrogator. He examined the faded stamp carefully and then handed it back to me and grinned half-heartedly as he said I was free to go. He seemed disappointed.

Nigeria 1975

Elephant Rocks

I loved night travel in Africa when you could have the road to yourself for hours on end. I would set off on a 300 to 400 mile drive mainly on dirt roads and never tire. I had a long wheel-based land rover and would settle myself for hours of dark silent travelling, a chain of cigarettes and my thoughts for company. There would be no traffic on the roads, none at all. I would start on metalled roads but before long would be driving on a dirt road, dry and dusty and ribbed. My headlights would cut a great swathe through the night, occasionally picking up the glinting eyes of some nocturnal creature on the prowl. Once on the dirt road – it was the dry season and the rains were not due for another month – the road would be ridged and potted. If you drove too slowly the endless ridges rattled you and, more important, they would rattle the vehicle to pieces. I had learnt by trial and error that the best speed for the land rover was between fifty and fifty-five miles an hour, fast enough for its wheels to skim straight from one ridge to the next without settling in the intervening ruts but to drive like that for hours on end required both skill and attention; the slightest variation in speed, a slowdown to avoid a pothole, and the land rover was bumping helplessly like a small vessel on a lake which unexpectedly encounters choppy water.

I loved the peace of those long night drives, my headlights picking out the bush to either side of the dirt road in strange distorted shapes so that, sometimes weirdly, it seemed as thought the trees were leaning over to enclose me in a ghostly glade. It was nonsense, a trick of the lights, but it gave an edge to the driving and made it more interesting. I had a box of fifty cigarettes, now much depleted, on the seat beside me and periodically I fumbled one-handed in the dark to extract a fresh smoke, then felt with my hand over the smooth leather until I located my lighter. All the while I did this I watched the road ahead, my right hand guiding the steering wheel while I kept the land rover skimming over the ridges at a steady fifty-five miles an hour.

I had just lighted another cigarette when I saw the great smooth rocks along both sides of the road – huge, rounded, grey-brown. There was something odd about them that drew my attention, causing me to hit a pothole. I skewed round dangerously so that by the time I had righted myself I was close to the edge of the bevelled surface near the deep drainage ditch. I braked sharply and then righted myself alongside another of the great rocks which towered above me. Only it wasn't a rock at all. It was an elephant. So were they all, a herd of them, night grazing. I was startled and frightened with my heart in my throat as I wondered what those ancient near primeval animals thought of the lighted monster that raced through the night. But they took no notice of me at all.

Central Africa 1966

The Great Pyramid – Giza

In September 1985 when I had just returned from a long trip in Africa I received a telephone call from the Foreign Office. A smooth voice asked whether I would be free to spend the next week in Cairo. Surprised – I had no links with the Foreign Office – I asked what they wanted me to do. There was a week's seminar for African diplomats taking place in Cairo – they never explained whether it was organised by Britain or by the Egyptian government – and it was felt that two sessions could/should be devoted to Britain in Africa. They knew I was an African 'specialist' and would I be prepared to give two talks (they called them presentations) and conduct subsequent seminars. Was there not someone at the Africa Desk of the FO who could do this? I asked but no, they wanted someone not connected with it. They could not offer me a fee but all my expenses for a week in Cairo would be met and half way through that week I would deliver my presentations. As it happened in all my travels to that date I had missed Cairo, which I certainly wanted to visit, and so I said yes.

Hesitantly, my FO contact said, "You won't be controversial, will you?"

I asked what he meant.

Well can you avoid talking about South Africa, which at that time was passing through a dangerously violent stage in the long battle against apartheid.

"I cannot talk about Britain in Africa without talking about South Africa which is at the top of the agenda." I said.

There was a sort of refined gulp over the line and my contact said, "Yes of course but – and he faded away.

I had a busy three days before leaving for Cairo and through a friend of mine who was in the FO I got the story. Mrs Thatcher was visiting the Middle East that week – Egypt and Jordan – and the FO wanted to demonstrate that they were engaged in aiding Africa in case she asked. I was the aid!

I enjoyed Cairo. I visited all the main sights and ate well and delivered my two speeches in which to the astonishment of my diplomatic audience I attacked the British stand on South Africa, a line that had clearly not been expected. At the end of the week the diplomats and myself were invited by our Egyptian host who had been in charge of the week's activities to come with him to a special supper that had been arranged in a hotel near Giza and the Sphinx. This was followed by a son et lumiere at the Sphinx. Then we wandered round the Great Pyramid of Cheops. It was of course dark but there were lights from the hotel for tourists that encroached on the grounds round the pyramids and the Great Pyramid stood black and awe-inspiring against the stars. So many superlatives had been used to describe it that I do not venture to add my own. Five thousand years old, consisting of 2,300,000 perfectly fitting stone blocks, some weighing as much as 16 tonnes it remains the greatest monument ever created by man.

I stood beside it in the dark looking up at its huge silent mass and could have remained like that for an hour when I became aware of our host standing beside me.

"It is the world's greatest marvel", he said, and I nodded assent.

"You admire it" and he put a query into his voice.

"Yes indeed" I said.

"You have nothing like it in Britain" he probed.

To this I readily agreed but added, defensively, "Our oldest monument is Stone Henge."

I knew that he knew all about Stone Henge. He shook his head as though worried by a fly while I only wanted to be left alone with my thoughts beside Giza but his determination to use the Great Pyramid to score a point over an Englishman broke the sense of ancient power that the pyramid had conveyed to me. I went with my host to our bus.

Egypt 1985

Baksheesh

I set off at seven in the morning on the two-day bus journey from Khartoum to Port Said. A small bribe ensured a good seat while oranges and unleavened bread were my standby for food. There had just been a coup and soldiers were everywhere in evidence. The bus, to my astonishment, set off on time and we soon discovered that its air conditioner was broken so that the only relief from the sweltering heat was the breeze from the small open windows. We stopped that night at Kassala whose backdrop of stark rocks rising like border sentinels to separate us from Ethiopia created one of the most spectacular African settings I knew. The little hotel was not unpleasant except for the latrines, which were to be avoided. The market took on a new lease of life with the dark and I wandered round it for an hour, fortified by drinks of orange accompanied with an equal proportion of ice and whirled in mechanical mixing machines until a sudden whining noise accompanied by the flickering and dying of the lights warned the town that the generator had malfunctioned. It did so, I learnt, on average twice a day.

Halfway on the second day we stopped by a sprawling roadside teahouse, which consisted of a series of huge awnings joined to one another to provide shelter for about forty tables. The kitchen was in the centre and large pans of spiced lamb or chicken stew gave off enticing odours. I found a small table and ordered a dish of raw onions, peppers, olive oil and unleavened bread and a bottle of Pepsi, which almost unbelievably in the intense heat was icy cold. I began to relax over this feast but then the beggars came. There was a gang of them, organised to come one at a time to my table. They had waited until the passengers from the bus had found tables and ordered food. Then they set about them. I was the only European travelling on that bus so was a natural target and regarded as a source of unlimited baksheesh. They came to me, one after another, evenly spaced as if they were under orders. I had some rapidly dwindling small change but though only one beggar at a time came to my small table, once he had gone another materialised at once. If for a moment I concentrated upon my food a cupped hand would appear slightly below the level of my nose:

"Baksheesh Baksheesh" came the wail. It was astonishing how many modulations or refinements could be injected into that one word.

But I knew there was more to come for I had become conscious of a giant beggar with a wooden leg ending in an iron stump who had remained at the far end of the open-sided tent. He, I was sure, was the master beggar who controlled the rest. He was truly a giant with massive shoulders, a barrel of a chest and a great close-shaved head. The wooden stump in place of a right leg only served to emphasise his strength. After the eighth beggar had left me I ordered a little glass of sweet tea while waiting for the call to the bus. Suddenly, the one-legged giant was beside my table:

"Baksheesh." He spoke with perfunctory arrogance as though his request would automatically be met. I ignored him.

"Baksheesh" and his voice rose a decibel. I shook my head negatively.

"Baksheesh, baksheesh".

Again I shook my head and added, "I have none".

"Baksheesh", his voice had now become peremptory.

I put my hand in my pocket and took it out and showed it to be empty in a universal gesture.

"Baksheesh, baksheesh" and now it was almost a roar. I shook my head again and managed to show distinct irritation at the same time.

"What do you mean, no baksheesh?" and his voice rose in a ferocious whining crescendo, a sort of tremolo of outrage. By this time we formed a central tableau and people at the adjoining tables were enjoying the show.

"No baksheesh" I said firmly. The giant now adopted different tactics and bent forward over my table to give a last roar of "baksheesh" but I said no backsheesh in a clear sharp voice. People at the nearby tables were smiling, some laughing and it was evident that the beggar was well known and not liked. Suddenly aware of this he leaned forward in one last threatening gesture to roar a final "baksheesh" into my face before turning to stump away. The giant's fury, which he usually simulated for effect, was real, made worse by the obvious enjoyment of the other spectators. The bus was now ready to depart.

Sudan 1988

A Turning Point

It was a lonely dirt road, full of freshly enlarged potholes after heavy rains. There was no sign of a village, no side roads, nobody and nothing except thick bush that stretched seemingly for ever on either side of me. I concentrated upon avoiding an especially large pothole. And then I saw the man who had suddenly materialised, perhaps 100 yards ahead. He was old. He wore a battered trilby hat that sat naturally on his head, as though it had always been there. His shirt, bleached from sun and endless washing, looked ready to fall apart. His grey flannel trousers, cast-offs that were too large for him, were held up by a piece of twine. An ancient pair of shoes clung to his feet – he wore no socks. He peered at my land rover, trying to discern my features through the windscreen. I knew the moment he saw that I was white. He moved to the side of the road and then turned to look inwards as I passed. He removed his hat as a sign of respect and held it against his chest. Then, as I came abreast of him he bowed his head. I drove on and as I did so I reflected that if our colonialism had reduced the people for whom we claimed responsibility to such a level of subservience then the sooner we left Africa to its own devices the better.

Africa 1964

Camels

Siad Barre was clinging onto power but his days were clearly numbered. I was staying with a red-haired Scottish friend of mine – a Macdonald naturally – and we had been visiting an aid project for which he was responsible.

We were driving southwards along the coast road back to Mogadishu. To our right were sand hills and dunes, to our left, sometimes in sight, the sea. We were not driving fast and could see clearly ahead of us on the roadside a lean-to shelter occupied by a solitary old man. As we approached he beckoned us to stop. It was a friendly gesture achieved by a sweep of the arm as though he was assigning the surrounding territory to us.

There was nothing to distinguish him – his shirt and trousers had seen much wear – except only his face seamed with many lines that testified to a long, possibly turbulent life. He inclined his head with a salaam of welcome and indicated the small fire behind him over which a contrivance of sticks held an enamel jug in which water was boiling. Three small tea glasses were arranged on a board that acted as a table. It was as though we were expected guests. We descended from our Landrover and salaamed in our turn.

Our host took the jug off the fire and groped in a little linen bag from which he extracted a handful of tealeaves to drop into the jug. He indicated a log on which we could sit and then he asked us how we liked his country. There is an art to answering such questions and we were both skilled in it and talked for his benefit. He was amused, there is no other way of describing his polite attention to what we said. Meanwhile he had filtered the tea into the three glasses, added sugar to a third of each glass's capacity and we sipped tea. Our host looked at each of us in turn then said the one word "aid" to my friend Macdonald.

"Yes" he replied and the old man nodded contentedly.

I was sitting, back to the road, in such a position that I could see the sand hills that rose steeply to a ridge that ran parallel to the road. A herd of camels was being led along the ridge, grunting their strange noises that sometimes reached us. It was difficult to judge but I thought the herd numbered about fifty. As far as I could make out the great camels were controlled by a man and a boy.

"You like my camels" the old man asked in excellent English.

"Is that your herd?" I asked.

"One of them" he replied, "I have three herds, it is time for them to be shipped to Yemen where the market is good this year."

"You must be a rich man", I said, "to own three such herds as this one." But the old man had turned his attention to my Scottish friend.

"Where do you live in Mogadishu", he asked, gentling his voice so as not to appear rude or inquisitive.

Iain told him and the old man nodded: "The houses in that road are reserved for foreigners – expatriates" he added but had difficulty with the word. He paused reflectively. Then, "I own three houses like yours" and he nodded at my friend.

Enjoying the impression he was making, the old man expanded. "Aid brings wealth to us. I do not live in such houses, of course, I rent them out to people like you. Foreigners like to live in those big houses." We rose to go and shook hands in European style before getting into our Landrover. Enlightened we took our leave and headed for Mogadishu. One can never be sure where wealth is to be found.   **Somalia 1990**

Locked in the Lavatory

Whenever I visited Karia – in those days I made an annual Africa trip – I would call upon my old friend Gustavus. He was a millionaire with a fortune derived from gold and diamonds that his uitlander grandfather had acquired in the mad rush to the Rand in the last quarter of the 19th century. Gustavus' fortune was inherited – he was no pioneer – but to secure his position in the new Africa he had married a black Princess.

When he made a remark about political instability, I asked: "Are you going to stay here permanently?"

I had slipped the question in while he was in full spate and so I got a direct, almost complete answer before he had time to think.

"When I have finished making my pile .....Doing my bit for Karia's development I mean, then I shall return to England."

He ignored the faint smile which his slip had occasioned and we talked of other things. He invited me to lunch on the coming Sunday when I could meet his little son Bogie although the Princess was away. Why he had chosen to call the boy Bogie – the gee was soft – I cannot imagine but Bogie it was and Gustavus spoke of him with immense pride.

"I am afraid you will have to take pot luck he said, "something cold." He always insisted that his servants – all of them – should have Sundays off so they could attend church. It was a gesture to liberal-paternalism though he himself rarely set foot inside a church.

"The food will be cold, I am afraid". he added again as I left.

The superior parts of Karia's capital consisted of mansions set in their own grounds in an area surrounding what had been the colonial governor's residence, now the State House of the President. Gustavus, needless to say, had one of these houses on what was still only half jokingly referred to as 'millionaire's row'. It was a grand bungalow house set in an acre of ground surrounded by high walls. I had driven slowly along the tree-lined road looking for it – the entrances all looked much the same and the others that I passed each had guards lounging at the gates. But true to the obstinacies of his nature, Gustavus had sent all his servants off to church for the day and so I was obliged to get out of the car and open the elegant wrought iron gates which were six feet tall, heavy and spiked. I drove up the drive straight into a domestic crisis.

I walked onto the long veranda – pots of exotic plants now in bloom made it a wonderful place to sit – and called for Gustavus. There was no answer but from within came the bawls, muffled of a child in distress. Then Gustavus came hurrying through the room beyond the veranda from some inner corridor. He was quite unlike his usual suave self, flustered, wringing his hands, on the verge of panic. Another muffled scream came from within.

"What is it, Gustavus?" I inquired. Another high-pitched scream, this one designed to penetrate whatever was responsible for the muffling.

"Little Bogie, my little Bogie, has locked himself in the lavatory!"

By this time Gustavus was close to disintegration. We went through to the back of the house and came to the lavatory door. The screams had turned into a steady distressed sobbing.

"All right Bogie" Gustavus called through the door, "Daddy is here."

Clearly inflamed by this useless piece of information Bogie redoubled his screams and kicked the door. Gustavus was in no condition to act rationally.

He stood wringing his hands and repeating: "How can I get my little Bogie out? How can I get my little Bogie out?"

He seemed as much in need of reassurance as did Bogie who had relapsed into quiet sobbing.

"Is there a window?" I inquired and then, having told Bogie through the door what we were going to do, Gustavus led me at a trot outside the house and round to the lavatory window. This was at the side of the house and mounting a large rock – only one of us could do so at a time – I peered down through a small window criss-crossed with iron bars at the child below. He was a plump moon-faced little boy of light coffee coloured skin and big round blue eyes but now his face was streaked with tears and sweat. He stared up at me, lips trembling.

"Bogie" I said "I have come to get you out."

The different voice and face as well as the hope I offered had the effect of inducing a momentary lull in the screaming and sobbing which gave me a chance to find out from Gustavus just what was entailed.

Normally there was a large key in the lock and earlier a triumphant Bogie had succeeded in locking himself in. But when it came to getting out again he could not manage to reverse the process and despite half an hour of instruction by Gustavus from the other side of the door, in the end Bogie had only managed to take the key out of the lock to discover he could not even insert it again. He was only two and a half.

Bogie had gone silent while I inspected him but now Gustavus took my place and at once the sight of his father set the child off again. His redoubled howls were too much for my friend Gustavus:

"I cannot stand this any longer" he cried, "I must get help. Will you talk to him while I am gone?"

Without waiting for any reply he was off, running, head down, arms jogging as though at the beginning of a long distance haul, round the lawn to the front of the house and out of my sight. Just what help he sought I did not know but there was I at the lavatory window, with Bogie below to be comforted. I felt an immediate sense of relief at the disappearance of Gustavus; now, perhaps, something could be done. Action was required.

"Bogie, do you want to come out?" He continued to howl.

"Bogie!" I spoke sharply, "Would you like to come out now." My words half penetrated and he cocked his head on one side to peer up at me through his tears.

"Good" I nodded to keep his attention. "Do you want me to get you out now – before your Daddy gets back" I added, my natural sense of fun coming to the fore.

He nodded vigorously and then waited, quite silent, in anticipation.

"Right. Now I shall tell you what to do. Your father has gone away", I said as a reassurance. It seemed to work for I had his undivided attention.

"Listen to me carefully and do exactly what I say and I'll have you out in one minute." Bogie nodded seriously, waiting for my next order

The large key lay on the floor where he had dropped it in despair or rage once he found he could not get it into the lock again. I peered down at the lavatory pan – the seat was up – and pushed my arm through the lower right hand square of the barred window. I could only manage to get my arm through up to my elbow.

"Now Bogie, put the lavatory seat down." He did so obediently.

"Can you climb up on it?" I asked. He nodded, big-eyed but silent.

"Not yet" I said. "Pick up the key and whatever you do don't drop it." He picked up the key and grasped it firmly in his right hand.

"Now, up you get on the seat." At this order he nodded emphatically, clearly it was something he was in the habit of doing.

"Don't drop the key", I said and again he nodded firmly, entering into the spirit of our joint operation. Absorbed in the physical effort, all thought of further crying having passed, Bogie heaved his podgy little frame up until he stood on one side of the seat and then looked expectantly at me for further orders.

"Good" I said. "Careful now, hold up your hand with the key and let me have it." At full stretch Bogie could just reach the hand I had thrust between the bars and a moment later I had the key.

"Well done Bogie, I am coming round to let you out."

I did so and we went out hand in hand onto the front lawn. It was a lovely day and a beautifully kept lawn and little

Bogie, happy in his release, ran up and down and then from under a bush brought a handful of his treasures – odd shaped stones – which he held out to me.

"Ploay?" he asked and I agreed. Bogie led me to a small rockery at the side of the lawn that he insisted was his own.

"Ploay" he repeated several times, it was a word which obviously got results, and since my role in the ploaying apparently consisted solely of sitting on a large comfortable rock while Bogie busied himself with numerous stones which he set out round me, I had no objection although I was beginning to feel in need of my pre-lunch drink. Bogie became engrossed with the absolute concentration that belongs only to small children and fanatics though occasionally he addressed unintelligible remarks in my general direction. I waited for the return of Daddy Gustavus.

Perhaps ten minutes had passed – Bogie engrossed with his stones, me contemplating the garden and becoming thirsty – when Gustavus came back. He had, to use old military parlance, raised the countryside. What this meant in fact was to recruit three immensely smart, liveried servants from a neighbouring, even grander house than his own and bring them back, I could only surmise, in order to smash down the offending lavatory door.

Gustavus was a small man with a round-topped balding head who had looked old-young before his time but would remain the same for years into the future. He wore thick-lensed glasses through which his eyes bulged and had bowlegs that running, which he did awkwardly, served to accentuate. His complexion was always fresh like that of a boy who has just come in from playing some active game on the sports field and now it was covered with a film of perspiration. He had brought back formidable reinforcements.

He led the way up the drive, still running, the odd pumping motions of his arms like engine pistons propelling him forwards. He was puffing from his unusual exertions. He was followed by his neighbour's steward, his cook and his houseboy. His neighbour, so I gathered, had made his pile some time ago and insisted upon smartness. His three servants wore spotless whites adorned with shining brass buttons while the steward was distinguished by a double-breasted jacket that had two rows of brass buttons and gold epaulettes. He also sported a brilliant red sash. The cook wore his cook's tall cap. They trotted single file as though Gustavus was taking his string of horses out for Sunday exercise. The steward was two paces behind Gustavus, the cook two paces behind the steward and the houseboy two paces behind the cook.

The rockery where I sat and Bogie played was off to the side of the drive, maybe forty yards from the gate, so that we were not immediately in the line of vision of the rescue party. In any case, Gustavus had removed his glasses in fear that they might fall off with all the violent exercise. His face gleamed scarlet with effort. As he trotted up the drive Gustavus looked back over his shoulder to make sure that his team followed. They ran in step, their faces grave as only Africans can manage gravity in absurd situations. And then Gustavus caught sight of us.

He came to an abrupt, startled halt as his eyes widened and the three African servants piled into one another and just managed under the severe command of the steward not also to pile into Gustavus. People often talk about eyes popping out of someone's head – it is an expression I have used myself – but until that day I had never actually seen it happen. But it did happen now. Gustavus' eyes bulged until I really began to fear they would pop out of his head altogether as he stood stupefied at the head of his relief column. It was pure Gilbert and Sullivan.

"What – what's this? Bogie!" he cried and came galloping across the lawn. Bogie, absorbed in his stones, took no notice until his father seized and lifted him into a startled embrace. The three servants, no doubt feeling they ought to get a little more mileage out of this Sunday morning charade, came over as well. They wanted to hear the explanation. To say that Gustavus was merely astounded would be to do myself and my small part in the affair an injustice. He was flabbergasted. Bogie, wriggling one arm free of his father's embrace held out a pebble and said: "Ploay" and insisted upon being put down so that he could get back to his rockery. I now had everyone's undivided attention. The three servants lined up as though for pay but it was not pay they wanted, it was the story. By nightfall, with embellishments, it would have been repeated in every kitchen the length of millionaire's row.

"How on earth? – but Gustavus could not go on.

"Quite simple" I said and with the understatement for which I was famous I gave a two-sentence account of what had passed in his absence.

"We have been playing on the lawn for the past ten minutes" I concluded.

I will say of Gustavus that he showed no trace of embarrassment. He turned to his neighbour's three retainers and thanked them graciously for coming while they kept their features perfectly controlled before, in their turn, thanking the master for asking them. Then they took leave to return to their own duties while Gustavus, once more turned to his son who had been lost – in a manner of speaking – and had been found again. So engrossed did he become in Bogie that I had, gently, to remind him of his duties as a host.

"I think perhaps a drink" I murmured and at that Gustavus became himself once more.

I must say he did me proud for lunch, cold and servantless though it was. We began with a first class champagne.

Zambia 1973

2　CANADA

Cap'n Tinkess

It was the summer that I read the great books. I was the engineer on a small diesel-powered ferry which plied back and forth all day long between the mainland and an island in the middle of a Muskoka lake. The island was a gem of beauty but chiefly memorable for the incredible old men who swarmed all over it. I have no mechanical aptitude whatever as anyone who knows me will willingly testify but I can drive. The ferry's engine, however, was the simplest I have ever worked: not that I have worked many engines but in this case the routine attached to my job really was elementary, a fact that almost caused my downfall. But that is to anticipate.

I had got the job in Toronto when I had begun to despair of getting anything. The clincher in my interview, or so I fondly imagined, was my supposed mechanical aptitude derived from having served briefly as a machine gun officer during my National Service in Austria. A greyhound bus deposited me in the tiny one street town of northern Ontario – its lake district – and from there I still had a further twenty miles to go along a side road before reaching the lake where I was to work. I had no money left at all. I explained this to the taxi-driver who was happy to take me: he said he would claim his fare from the 'Inn on the Lake', my employer for the next four months.

When we reached the jetty the lake was choppy with white horses riding high; the sky was a deep blue, the sun bright and sharp, a May sun heralding the heat of the approaching Canadian summer. Small wisps of white cloud moved at speed across the sky, sometimes briefly obscuring the sun but only in the manner of a light lace curtain in its dancing progress across the heavens. Several wispy clouds would come together threatening to form a more impenetrable white cushion but then would break again, rejoin, as though in a ceaseless game of tag, finally to disperse in fragments which were wafted at speed into the distance before they disintegrated. A launch was tied to the jetty: the taxi driver had brought mail and other odd commissions for someone on the island and Marcel, a taciturn young Quebecois, took them and me on board.

We headed across two miles of lake towards a group of white wooden buildings at the shore's edge in the centre of the island. Otherwise trees came everywhere to the water, trees of a wonderfully rich deep green except where black outcrops of rock broke the general symmetry of the forest. The 'Inn on the Lake' consisted of a series of buildings widely separated from one another: there was an octagonal banqueting hall whose sides towards the lake went sheer into the water; a main reception hall and dining room but these were up a hill through the trees and out of sight of the lake; and the covered jetty where we now docked; boat sheds, maintenance staff quarters of which I discovered I was to be a part, canoe sheds. Hidden among the trees in the centre of the island were the junior staff quarters: log huts for the men, bungalows for the girls. There was an 18-hole golf course at one end of the island and an observation tower on the highest point. There were elegant "villas" for the guests. There were beaches for swimming – one for the guests, another for the staff. The island was designed to ensure relaxed 'country' luxury for its guests – at a price. Deep in the woods behind the male staff quarters was the staff dining room, somewhat grandly called a mess. All the buildings were of wood – the smart ones of the main hotel and guest lodges painted white and pointed in red; the staff buildings of rough hewn logs, cabin style.

It was a lovely island: a mile long, three miles round and half a mile wide. Except for the golf course and space round the buildings the rest was given over to a forest of pines and these remained largely undisturbed. Many years before a path had been cut round the shore of the island but this was now thickly overgrown and since the guests rarely showed any inclination to walk the manager did not waste staff labour clearing the undergrowth. Periodically, on my afternoons off, I would circle the island slashing at the undergrowth with a stick. The woods had become a bird sanctuary providing a home for a wide variety of woodpeckers. They were also full of racoons.

It was then early May and the season did not begin until mid-June. My task was to prepare the ferry, which meant painting it and otherwise helping with a variety of odd jobs. Later, I would become a full time engineer on ferry duty all day. Once it began in June the season lasted until early September. Except for certain regulars the hotel staff was recruited annually and consisted almost entirely of high school or university students earning summer pocket money or their next year's fees. All the waiters, waitresses, barmen, bellhops, maids or washers-up would be students. But the maintenance work was carried out by the old men. They formed a regular staff and almost all of them were then in their sixties or seventies and some, as I discovered, were older still. They had been coming to the island for years and for most of them this annual four-month stint – maintenance and preparations began a month before any guests were expected to arrive – appeared to be the highlight of their working lives.

The head of maintenance at perhaps fifty, an age which gave him at least a decade's advantage over the old men, was a permanent fixture on the island. This was George. He had a large bulbous nose with a huge wart gracing its left side, a close-cropped balding head and a raucous voice, which went with his red face. For some unaccountable reason – he came originally from Derbyshire – he was known to everyone as 'Willie the Greek' – though never to his face. His sidekick was a Yorkshire man and it was Keith who told me how all the old maintenance staff insisted that George was 'Willie the Greek'. Keith's official title was assistant maintenance superintendent while 'Willie the Greek' was the 'super' and it was Keith who instructed me in what became my main task for the next three weeks: painting the ferry.

The ferry was then housed in its winter quarters, a large boat shed where it was dry docked well clear of the water lapping below. Like George, Keith lived on the island year round and had already been there for ten years. He was a bachelor of about thirty- five and looked set to remain a lifer. In winter both men acted as general caretakers. The lake would freeze solid during the Canadian cold; Keith had a little Austin Seven on the island, which he could drive to the mainland across the ice in winter.

During those first days I painted, explored the island and talked with Keith about England: he spoke with great nostalgia although he had no intention of returning. Sometimes I worked on the scow with Bill, ferrying across the summer supplies. Occasionally George sent me on an errand in the launch with the taciturn Marcel, the youngest by far of the regulars, who did not allow that he should be regarded like them as an old timer. The summer had yet to settle and in grey cloud with high waves making the water rough, white horses running swiftly before us, Marcel and I would bump and ride over the water while the spray flew back to cover the thick glass windshield.

"See Marcel isn't stupid" George would say to me without elaborating what form the stupidity was likely to take. Marcel was taciturn because he could not speak English, none of the old men had ever learnt any French.

Gradually during this calm period before the summer rush I got to know the old men. They were happy to be referred to as old timers, like characters sitting perpetually on the sidewalks of American Westerns. My chief informant was Bill on the scow. I think his other name was Hancock though I never really found out. He had spent the whole of the 1914-1918 War in the trenches and he was full of stories about that gruesome yet compellingly nostalgic war, about his early struggles in Canada – he had come out under a scheme for discharged servicemen in 1920, he said; and about other old timers on the island.

"It's like a club here", he told me; "We've been coming to the island for years now. I was twenty-four when I emigrated to Canada and I've been coming to the island for thirty years." Bill had done all sorts of other odd jobs round Ontario, never with much success he admitted, though he was without either rancour or shame at his failures. He had no pretences but of the island he said: "I like it here. Peaceful!" For a moment he looked at me appraisingly: "I've seen some types too" he added, "they come and go."

Bill knew all the pubs round Charing Cross station; or rather, he had known the ones which were there during the First World War when he came to London on his all too brief leaves.

"We drank ourselves silly most of the time", he said. Together we checked to see if I knew the same pubs. "Couldn't afford to go back, ever" said Bill. I never discovered whether he was married or had any family in Canada. But year after year he returned to the "Inn on the Island".

Once these old men discovered I was English they would drift along to tell me their backgrounds. Proudly they disclosed what turned out to be no more than a nodding acquaintanceship, one generation removed, with a corner of rural England or a district of London. The carpenter, then well into his seventies, said his parents had been born within the sound of Bow Bells although he had been born in Muskoka and had never travelled farther than fifty miles in any directions from the area of the lake. He had seen London in pictures ands he spoke of it as his parents must have described it to him half a century earlier. His friend, another septuagenarian, was responsible for the boilers: his father came from Stonehouse in Gloucestershire. He was a Sherlock Holmes enthusiast and had read all the stories over and over. When he discovered I knew Baker Street he asked me to describe it in detail; I did so and he seemed disappointed as though he expected Hansom cabs still to use it.

Another of these old timers who certainly played up to his role was an Indian whose crag-lined face would have graced any Western. He was, they told me, for the Indian always maintained an impassive mien and did not speak at all, a pure Huron. The youngest of this curious collection of old men by-passed by time, a mere chicken of fifty-six, was a fat Scotsman whose principal occupation was looking after the island drains. He was always first in the staff food queue, waiting patiently for the cook's assistant to open the doors to our log dining room. In the four months I spent there he never once missed his post.

The doyen of these old timers was eighty-six. He was short, thickset, slightly hunchbacked though with age rather than as a deformity. His huge drooping moustaches looked to have been in place without change for half a century. As he walked his head nodded back and forth as though his neck was no longer strong enough to perform its control function and keep the head sufficiently firmly in place. None of the others remembered when he had first come to work at the Inn. His job was to maintain the polish of the great dance floor in the octagonal banqueting hall. Except for convention banquets, which were held there the hall was normally used for nightly dancing. He polished this floor with the aid of an electric polisher which he had referred to for years as a 'new invention'. This invention, which he plugged in at one corner of the hall, worked on a virtually limitless extension of flex. The difficulty by then was that the machine had taken over. Once the power was turned on it was all he could manage to hold on while the polisher described its own patterns across the floor. Gripping the handle with both hands he followed where the polisher led while his shoulders heaved steadily in rhythm with his instrument as though he had hiccups. Once during the summer, greatly daring, one of the young students asked him how this constant pulling motion affected him; he chuckled good-humouredly and said it helped 'contain his rheumatics'.

All these old timers – the entire maintenance staff, as far as I could judge – were British immigrants or descended from parent immigrants and had lived all their lives in the area. They were ancient if friendly failures for whom the Inn on the Island appeared to be the last post.

My ferry was named the Swallow – the third of a succession of that name which had worn out in crossing the lake. I became expert at applying coats of paint by the time I had the ferry ready for service: white all over but pointed in red, green and orange – the island colours. The ferry had an upper deck with seating arranged round the rails that acted as a backrest, as well as across the deck. The bridge was equipped with an elegant spoked wheel and looked down on a small forward deck carefully fenced off from wandering passengers. Six broad steps led back from the bridge down into the cabin area; in the middle of this in a glass windowed 'box' was the engine room. The engineer sat at what in effect was a small desk facing the steps and the captain at his wheel. On the right hand side of the desk were two silver levers with black knobs, the outside one to control forward, the inside lever to control reverse: a simple push-button started the engine (though that had yet to be installed) and the captain controlled the speed, stopping and starting by a system of bells. The ferry was designed to carry forty passengers comfortably with their baggage. Apart from the captain and the engineer one male student acted as porter and ticket collector: he loaded and off-loaded baggage, tied up at the jetties and went round on the journey selling tickets for the passage across the lake. The operation of this ferry, as I was to learn, could not have been more simple.

The students who were to form the bulk of the summer staff now began to arrive; they were mainly boys and girls in their late teens. They were a fresh-faced, rowdy, happy lot, and for about a week before the real season began when supposedly they were training they spent most of their time canoeing or swimming.

Then one day George told me that the ferry's engine was to be brought to the island the next day to be installed: it was removed each winter for an overhaul and would be fitted into the ferry by two company engineers. Early the next morning as I put the final touches to my paintwork I became aware of a squat silver-haired man with thick sensuous lips standing in the entrance to the boat house eyeing me and the ferry. I greeted him and he introduced himself as Captain Light. He had a silken voice and eyes that were incapable of settling anywhere even for a moment. I did not like him. Later, when I saw George, I mentioned that I had met the Captain.

"The Captain? You mean Light" and he spat the name out, "He's not the captain, merely the number two." His scorn was palpable. When George disapproved which was frequent enough he made no bones about it.

The engineers fitted the engine that afternoon. We were to have 'trials' as George put it the next day when I would be taught my duties as engineer.

In the staff dining room at supper I saw a diminutive little man sitting between George and Keith: they were at the other of our two long trestle tables with their backs to me. I finished my meal, lit a cigarette and was preparing to leave when George called me over.

"This" he said with emphasis "is the Captain: Captain Tinkess. He will be in charge of the ferry all summer." Now that I was face to face with Cap'n Tinkess, for the abbreviated form of his title was used by everybody except 'Willie the Greek', I could hardly believe that he could or should be employed. He was minute, perhaps five foot four inches in height, a tiny thin waif of a man. His face was lined and wrinkled, as any true captain's face ought to be, his hair grizzled and short-cropped, his eyes a rheumy, watery brown while attached to the end of his nose as a permanency was a large drip which never fell and was never tackled by the Captain. For so small a man he gave me a surprisingly big hand to shake and his grip retained a strength that belied his years.

"Cap'n Tinkess is eighty-two" said Keith with pride.

"Eighty-three" the Cap'n corrected.

The Cap'n's powers of conversation were strictly limited: indeed, apart from monosyllables which were his favourite means of communication – and these he avoided if possible – he rarely spoke at all, at least not with the other staff. The ladies: that was different.

"You will be going out together tomorrow" George said, "Keith and I will come too." I was dismissed.

Old Bill was hovering at the door when I left, hankering for a bit of gossip.

"Tell me about the Cap'n" I asked him.

"Aah" he replied with considerable feeling, "old Tinkess has been coming here longer than any of us. He captained the other boats before this one; he's done it since before the First War. I hope you treated his ferry right" he said, "It's his pride and joy. You had better have painted it well" Bill added with a sly grin, "he'll inspect it closely tomorrow, you see."

Cap'n Tinkess always dressed the same: he wore a blue serge uniform with a double-breasted coat close-buttoned with large brass buttons always beautifully shone, a peaked cap that bore the insignia of the hotel and emerging elegantly from his right cuff an immaculate white handkerchief which he never used. Tucked into his breast pocket was a yellow handkerchief sometimes brought out with a flourish but certainly never employed to remove the drip from the end of his nose. The captain's noted taciturnity as well as his age meant he was left much to himself which he liked. He had assumed an accepted position of superiority in relation to all the other old men – including the eighty-six year old 'jigger' from the dancehall – but that was by reason of his longer tenure of a post on the island. That whole summer I cannot recall exchanging more than a "good morning" or "good night" with him, not even when the crisis came. My crisis, that is. The Cap'n had one other distinguishing feature: his drooping eyelids. With his ancient face these gave him the constant appearance of being on the verge of sleep. Yet when he saw a pretty girl a tiny, quaint little smile would hover round his lips to light up his face. The Cap'n always appeared on the jetty an exact five minutes before our stints began and though there were never any alterations in his appearance or dress sometimes he had failed to synchronise the buttons of his jacket so that one side was a button distance lower down than the other side. No one liked to tell him when he had got his buttons wrong. Otherwise his appearance was impeccable.

Once that summer when one of the girl students had come on board while we were alongside the jetty – she was Al the porter's current flame – Cap'n Tinkess, his eyelids drooping more than usual in sympathetic expectation, came up behind the girl with a frisky little action – almost but not quite a jump – to pull her floppy summer hat down over her eyes from behind. For so small and ancient a man he showed sudden bounces of extraordinary youthful high spirits.

He had a daughter of about fifty who taught school in the little town where the road to the lake turned off from the main highway. Once a week the Cap'n went to see her and whenever the time came for his visit he became excited and his face would light up in expectation. On one occasion when George handed him a letter he looked at the writing on the envelope and then exclaimed "Oh my daughter" in a kind of ecstasy. His wife, Bill told me, was only eighty but more aged than her husband and shaky on her legs though still game. Occasionally when for some reason our schedules got mixed up I would do a spell with Light – I never referred to him as Captain – and once we took Tinkess across to his daughter who was waiting with her car on the mainland to take him off for the afternoon. Her features were exact reprints of her father's down to the drooping eyelids and rheumy eyes: only the nose drip was missing.

We took the Swallow out the next day. Gently she rolled down to the water, Cap'n Tinkess at the wheel, Keith at the engine with me beside him for instruction. George came to supervise the run as did the two engineers who had installed the engine the previous day. Light came along although nobody took any notice of him though he kept talking. The other 'engineer' who would spell me had not yet arrived: or rather, as Keith whispered to me, the Mounties had picked him up for some serious crime just after he had signed on so as yet there was no one else to work with me. "If they cannot find someone else you will get paid double" Keith informed me and though the prospect of a sixteen hour day was somewhat daunting I could certainly do with the money.

We made a complete circuit of the island and out in the deeps we practised. All I was required to do was press the starter button and then manipulate my two levers forwards or backwards, as I had been shown by Keith, in response to the Cap'n's bells. It was extremely simple: one ring was for half speed in either starting or slowing down; two bells for full speed ahead; three bells for reverse. Once Keith had explained these intricacies to me I took over the driving seat, or rather, the engineer's seat, and the Cap'n went through the bell routine twice: I slowed, full-steamed ahead and reversed. The engineers pronounced themselves satisfied, Keith and George pronounced me trained and we returned to the covered jetty where the ferry was now to dock for the rest of the summer. There I had to answer the reversing bells in earnest as the Cap'n brought us in.

The next day we had our inspection, The launch was sent across to the mainland at noon to pick up the inspector who was taken to lunch in the main hotel by the manager: Murchison, who had hired me in Toronto on the strength of my machine gun knowledge, had arrived two days earlier and the Inn was now more or less ready for the beginning of what everyone claimed would be a busy season. After lunch we went aboard for another circuit of the island but this time a much larger contingent accompanied us.

The inspector was short and stout, balding and bespectacled, pompous and self-important and – apparently – humourless. He was a Scotsman. He began his inspection before we took to the lake and was followed round the ferry by the manager, the assistant manager, George and Keith, the two maintenance engineers, Cap'n Tinkess and Mr. Light. I brought up the rear.

When the inspector said: "You need another fire-fighting appliance here" one appeared as though by magic from behind someone's back. When he entered my small engine room everyone attempted to crowd in behind him only to pile out again when he turned round. When he stopped to look at something, my paintwork for example, the following file piled up like soldiers halted too abruptly. And so, strung out behind him and trying to anticipate the queries he would pose, we followed him up and down the length of the little ferry: on the top deck, on the captain's bridge, back in the passenger cabin. At any criticism he made all hastened to agree that whatever the faulty part improvements would at once be carried out. The manager would look at George, George at Keith and Keith – because no one was left more lowlier than he – at me. Then in an upsurge of babble everyone would hasten to suggest his own remedy to achieve the desired end. At one point the inspector essayed a joke: it was a poor but lofty official joke and as realisation came upon us that it was a joke a nervous laugh echoed round the circle into which we had formed.

Then he gave the signal for us to go and as on the previous day we circled the island. This time Cap'n Tinkess didn't do any of the bell practice – that had been entirely for my benefit – and the inspector sat contentedly on the top deck enjoying the breeze. An hour later, after a wide circuit, we docked. Satisfied with his performance the inspector finally sat down in a chair thoughtfully brought on deck by George who was flourishing his habitual large red silk handkerchief to mop his brow. The inspector took out his docket of papers to write out the annual certificate of sea or rather lake-worthiness. This he did slowly and ponderously. All gathered round to watch, waiting to approve his next joke but, more important, to take possession of the certificates as he completed them in fear that otherwise he might change his mind and not issue any at all. They must have gone through the same ritual year after year.

"That inspector" Keith whispered to me "has been coming for a decade at least"; he had been the inspector throughout Keith's ten years on the island and every year they were just as nervous, he told me. "He's a tricky one," he added. Throughout the inspection each had maintained his prescribed hierarchical place: the manager at the inspector's elbow, George next to him, Keith next to George and the rest of us grouped in a half circle round the chief actors. It would have been a disaster for the Inn had the inspector refused a certificate for any reason: no guests! And he knew it; he enjoyed his power to the full.

Perhaps, after all, he did have a sense of humour for his deliberative slowness and many pauses kept his court on their toes for half an hour. This certainly pleased him but had it also amused him? Of that I could not be sure. I, too, received a certificate, which qualified me as a 'diesel engineer second-class temporary for service on the Ontario lakes'.

By then it was early June and the first guests were trickling in although we were still nearly empty. None the less, George put the ferry on full schedule. Our regular crew consisted of four: the Cap'n and myself, and Al and Pete who alternated with each other as crew. Al was a big gangling boy of seventeen just out of high school; he was good-natured, cheery, courteous and immensely attractive to the girls who all chased him. He was not overmuch endowed with wits. Pete on the other hand was two years older, short and fat; he also had just finished high school. Pete was vague as to whether he would go on to university. But whereas Al was easy going Pete was a bustler who liked to organise others. And he was mean about the tips. Another engineer had been found at the last moment so I did not have to do the job as Keith had suggested for sixteen hours a day. My alternate, Jim, was Irish: about fifty and normally quiet and steady, he would indulge in a sudden blind about once a month when I would take over his day for him. Then I was obliged to work with Light. He would use the opportunity to make disparaging remarks about Tinkess, suggesting through his wet lips that the old man was really past it but always ending "I like Tinkess, I want to help him – and you." He spent his days spreading poison.

The routine was simple and unchanging: Cap'n Tinkess rang his bells from the bridge, I worked my levers. I timed the trip across the lake: an average run took fourteen minutes and we did a full circle once an hour. We started at eight in the morning from the island and fourteen minutes later docked at the mainland jetty to take on passengers. We would begin the return journey at eight-thirty, the round commencing again at nine o'clock. The two crews worked from eight to twelve and then eight to midnight one day and midday to eight in the evening the next. In my off time I explored the island, swam, sunbathed and read. I got through more reading that summer than at any other time that I can remember. On an average fourteen-minute trip I reckoned on twelve minutes reading. The other two minutes were spent in starting and stopping although to say so makes the process sound more complex than it was in reality. My reading habits became a matter of conversation among the old men and still more among the students who by and large appeared not to reckon reading highly. Old Tinkess never said a word but then he hardly ever said a word about anything.

Sometimes if an especially large group of guests used the ferry together I would help load or offload the luggage. Then Al would cheerily insist upon sharing with me any tips he received. But Pete would stuff the tips into his jeans pocket and look away. On one occasion when the members of a convention all departed together even Cap'n Tinkess helped with the luggage and one of the guests, no doubt acting for the rest, stuffed a handful of notes into chubby Pete's greedy hands – unfortunately it was his day on duty. Chubby Pete looked at us but made no offer. Cap'n Tinkess hooded his eyes lower than usual, otherwise staring blankly in Pete's general direction. I knew he disapproved.

"What of us Chubby, the Cap'n and I did half your work for you?" I stood in front of him waiting. Pink-faced he turned a grudging back on me, fumbling the notes in his hands; then he handed two dollars each to me and the Cap'n though he had been given at least twenty. I looked at the Cap'n and shrugged. I thought I detected the faintest hint of a shrug in return but certainly no more: its very faintness all but defeated its purpose. Communication was not the Cap'n's strong point.

I was sealed off from the passengers in my glassed engineer compartment but those who decided to sit in the aft cabin had to pass along a passage beside me. In passing they always peered in: at me; at the engine or rather the neat desk at which I sat with my two silver levers with their black knobs and the starter button for those constituted the only visible engine; or at what I was reading. I had become used to the deafening noise in my glass cage and the sight of the Cap'n's back up on the bridge. The passengers I ignored. I simply read. The setting was idyllic; the job simple; and I had brought with me plenty of books, which I found I was devouring at a remarkable rate. I could not hear the passengers round me through the glass because of the hum of the engine: at most, even when the cabin was crowded, their talk formed no more than a faint background babble. But they would peer over my shoulder through the glass partition or come to the side to read the title of my book. If they did not see the titles they raised their eyebrows and went away. They used to question Al about the 'egghead you have as an engineer'.

I had made a book cover of thick brown paper, which transferred from book to book; my object was to hide the title so as not to excite their comments. My device did not work as I had planned since it was assumed that the brown cover hid works of pornography. On one occasion when I had shut my book to slow the engine a tourist who was slightly drunk tapped insistently on the glass at the side by my head pointing at my book and repeatedly mouthing: "What are you reading" as he leered knowingly at the brown cover. After three taps – he was beginning to get aggressive – I shrugged and opened the book at the title page: it was Berkeley's "A New Theory of Vision". That certainly shut him up and his leer changed into a sort of bewildered dismay. He retreated to the back of the cabin where I sensed rather than saw him trying to explain how my book had not turned out to be pornography at all. On another such occasion I was reading the Koran.

By early June the Inn on the Island was full: clients divided about equally between weekend golfers and fishermen or conventions. The guests were the worst part of the whole affair; without them the island would have been a little paradise for us workers. Most of the staff were young students while a high proportion of the guests, the majority, were middle-aged men usually coming for conventions, sometimes accompanied by their wives. They had plenty of money and tipped generously but they were patronising, full of clever remarks for the young staff and too often would chase lewdly after the girls. Few appeared to possess the 'gravitas' which might have been expected to go with their age. The old timers were collectively scathing about them and so were most of the students. Luckily I had no contact with them at all except through my glass partition and the sound of the engine, which at first I had cursed, I now blessed since it effectively made impossible any conversations through the glass. I lived in my world of the 'great books'.

The island and its mixed population presented some curious contrasts. There was a kind of innocence about the place: the old men with their memories, now safely in retreat from the real world; Cap'n Tinkess lighting up with pride and pleasure when he went off to his daughter; and the students full of fun and nonsense determined to enjoy their summer's work. Only the fat-bellied weekend golfers coming to get away from their wives or the conventions whose excuse usually was to drink without the golf struck an unpleasant chord. No one, of course, could afford the Inn unless he had plenty of money – it was in no sense cheap. And the big profits came from the cheap labour on which the operation depended.

The man who owned the Inn on the Lake was a millionaire called Lester. He spent most of July and August there though he had business interests all over Canada. Lester ran his hotel on the basis that either he employed his old crocks at a pittance until they dropped – the island was summer home to most of them and other employment would have been difficult to come by; or he employed students whom he sacked at the slightest excuse, more were always to be found. He was mean by nature and mean in his operations. Most staff were taken on for a period of three months but their wages were split in two parts: they were paid a portion at the end of each month; the other portion was kept back as a bonus to be paid as a lump sum at the end of the season dependent upon their good behaviour and whether or not they completed the summer. There was some justification for this system since many of the students were notoriously lax about completing their engagements and this was one way of ensuring that staff remained for the busiest part of the summer. But Lester, as I learnt from Al who was a fund of information, spent the last weeks of the summer as business began to fall off finding excuses to sack as many students as he could for trifling offences. He would do this when they only had a few more days to complete their contracts so depriving them of their bonuses.

Lester was always on the prowl. He considered his main duty was to protect the good reputation of the girls since their parents might visit the island and he was not going to have any pregnancies. The girls who suffered from his attentions had a good deal to say about the quality of his protection.

And then 'Big Dave' arrived. He was a gorilla of a man: six foot six, about 40, an ex-wrestler, ex-body-builder, huge muscled and thick headed. By then he was beginning to go to seed and possessed a vast wrestler, beer-drinking stomach. He came as the island guard but his main function was to make sure the students stayed in their quarters at night. He prowled round their huts checking the windows. Lester was not drinking that year – normally he drank heavily – and this made him extra mean. He watched the girls all the time. On one occasion at about two in the morning I was awakened by a terrifying roar. I looked out of my window – my quarters were above the jetty where the ferry docked – to see that Dave had caught two students, a boy and a girl, sneaking in late in a borrowed canoe. The boy was a big husky lad of maybe nineteen, a nice solid football player, but he was dwarfed by 'Big Dave' and when the latter roared at him to sit down he sat down like a scared ten-year old. Meekly. And sensibly. Dave's great roar became a feature of the island although he was careful not to roar near the guest lodges. Once he roared upon a couple in the woods at three in the morning but only the girl was a staff student, the man was one of the guests. The girl was sacked the next day. Dave's roar sounded through the Canadian pines all that summer like a Moose in the rutting season.

Apart from his official night duties Dave was a harmless overweight buffoon. He had been all over the world wrestling or chucking out. He had chucked out in London, Milan, Cape Town, Sydney, Singapore, Macao, Hong Kong, San Francisco and New York. The students soon learned how to manage

Dave. He was brain damaged from wrestling or chucking out or both and what he really liked to do was spend the day at the staff beach showing off to the students. "I've been teaching the kids how to jack-knife", he would say as he came dripping along the wooden causeway towards his quarters.

Normally on my afternoons off – every other one – I went to a retreat of my own. About a mile round the island along the overgrown path a large black rock jutted into the lake, the water lapping thirty feet below. No one ever came there although occasionally canoes passed round the point, hugging the shore. I spent many hours reading on my rock and swimming in the limpid waters. The rock was exposed on a corner of the island and the slightest wind would cause a whistling in the pines and make the leaves flap and crackle.

The Iraq crisis in the Middle East dominated the news but seemed remote to us on our lake although Keith whose loyalty to Britain and principally Yorkshire was unwavering claimed that the Royal Navy was there: it is the largest in the world, he assured me, and had never been beaten. I passed the summer in reading and other excitements were few and these composed of breaks in the routine. There was the evening when I was awakened by Keith at ten thirty just after falling into a deep sleep because Jim the Irish engineer had hit the bottle and was uncontrollable. So I took the ferry from him until midnight while he promised me a month's wages for bailing him out. Another day the cook down at the staff mess found a huge old racoon in the dustbin. We had racoon stew for days afterwards: it was tasty and a general improvement on our normal fare but I preferred the racoons alive in the woods for they are among the most friendly of creatures.

At lunchtime and in the early evenings a four-piece band would play on the sundeck which faced the lake. I could see this band from my engine room across the water: one man plucking a double bass, a second at the piano, the third swaying to his accordion and the fourth with his saxophone or his rattlers as they jigged in time to their rhythms. They wore white ducks, red jackets, white shirts and red bow ties and dark glasses. They jigged and smiled looking inanely sophisticated but from my distance it was all mime, a silent coloured television screen facing the lake. Normally I kept the window on the lakeside of my engine room open and occasionally when the wind played tricks a single note might be carried across the water to me despite the noise of the engine – a plaintive wail from the saxophone or a twang from the double bass – but then they would resume their mime.

Then came my 'accident' or 'crisis' as I prefer to call it.
By this time I had become known as 'the Englishman who reads those books'. The adjective *those* managed to convey something special about the quality of the books which I was reputed to read: they were highbrow, intellectual, deep. Al told me all this. Al got the gossip from the girls or, rather, from the particular girl he was going with that week. And he fed them with information about me – or rather, about my books. He would come to find out the title of my latest book and ask me to tell him what it was about. I mention this because my reading was the cause of the crisis.

As I have said the engine was the simplest I have ever worked; so simple in fact that I could conveniently ignore it while I read for the entire length of each crossing. I took the engine for granted which was all right in its way since it gave no trouble. Unfortunately, I came to take the bells for granted too. Normally my response was mechanical and without taking an eye from the printed page my two hands would reach out to my right side in answer to the bells and I would pull or push the levers, back or forth, together or separately, whatever was appropriate. But finally on this near disastrous occasion there was no response – mechanical or otherwise – from me at all.

I suppose I did register the bells but only dimly at the back of my mind and very dimly at that for I was deeply engrossed in my reading. On looking back it is interesting that I cannot for the life of me remember what it was that I read with so much absorption. Gradually, however, bells began to register, more bells than normal: not just the two for slowdown which I had been expecting and had missed but half-a-dozen somehow imbued with a sense of urgency. Still I read on. Then came non-stop bells and sudden alarm made me look up. Cap'n Tinkess on his bridge above me was no longer just a back and a peaked cap; he was running towards me, or rather dancing up and down on his little old legs, waving his arms in a kind of desperation, a look of horror and despair on his face. I think he had been shouting too but I had heard nothing above the noise of the engine.

The end of the jetty with the great beam which held the covering roof was flashing past my window – the ferry used to come in straight towards one end of the dock with the jetty to the side so that if we overran the prow would meet solid wood beams on a rock base which had no give in it whatsoever – and we were still going at full speed. So much for my automatic responses. I grabbed my two levers and crashed the engine into full reverse. We shuddered the length of the dock creating four-foot waves which swept over it and splashed all round; they also did much to slow the ferry as they rocked it madly from side to side. As it happened the engine was in excellent order and withstood this violent reverse manfully – thanks to the two engineers and the inspector. And luckily for me, for some purely fortuitous reason, there was not a single passenger aboard. Al who was on duty had gone onto the upper deck where he was contentedly sitting enjoying the breeze and the rapidly approaching docks without any apparent misgivings: as he told me later he "had just thought we were coming in rather fast" until the sudden reverse had almost jerked him off into the water.

We did hit the end of the dock but by then had almost slowed to normal tying up speed. There was a dull booming clunk of wet wood on wet wood. We rocked violently and for another thirty seconds waves continued to splash heavily up the sides of the ferry and wash across the empty jetty. Then as if to register a protest at such treatment a single complete pane of glass from one of the square windows of the passenger cabin alongside me fell slowly inwards to shiver into fragments on the deck. For a moment there was silence except for the heavily lapping water. Then all hell broke loose; or more precisely, 'Willie the Greek' followed by Keith came storming aboard. Out of the corner of my eye I saw them erupt onto the bridge, George shouting and Cap'n Tinkess gesticulating but I made a pretence of struggling with the levers. I had the wit to whisk my book out of sight behind the co-pilot's seat, which was never occupied. A moment later Keith was beside me demanding "What in God's name….."

"The levers got stuck Keith, I cannot imagine ….."

"Stuck!" snarled George who had followed Keith down, leaving Cap'n Tinkess standing calm and impassive on his bridge where Al had at last appeared to demand what was happening.

George spent the next minute swearing. I gathered gradually that George and Keith had been standing on the quay quite idly – though they did not use that expression – when they suddenly realised the speed at which the ferry was approaching and had been shouting at Tinkess from the dock. As luck would have it the day was dull and overcast and no guests were waiting to cross to the mainland; indeed, hardly anyone was about at all, another aspect of my good fortune. With commendable foresight I had taken up a standing position, both hands glued to my little silver levers with their black knobs, so that it really did look as though I had been doing desperate battle to reverse the engine.

"It's those damned books you keep reading", shouted George purple with fury.

"The levers got stuck George." I too, like Tinkess, maintained an impassive air. George looked round furiously for my current book but none was in sight. He glared at Keith:

"Get the tools and strip the bloody engine down; find out what is wrong. The ferry can't go until we are sure." Keith scuttled ashore for his tools. I sat back and copying George with his big silk handkerchief mopped my brow as though we had all come through a formidable engineering crisis together. Keith returned with his bag of tools and George stumped off.

There were no trips for two hours. Keith stripped the workings right down, checking the levers which were beautifully oiled and in splendid working condition. For decency's sake I hung around for a while but then – as I had often told Keith that I had no mechanical aptitudes and there seemed no point in my presence – I went ashore and up to my room which overlooked the jetty anyway. There I read another book but every ten minutes or so I looked out of the window to see how Keith was progressing. On the last occasion that I did so Cap'n Tinkess, who had disappeared while the engine inspection was carried out, was now back on his bridge.

I came onto the dock from my room, careful not to be carrying a book. George looked at me suspiciously:

"It's those damned books", he growled making them sound like some form of living obscenity. There were still no passengers waiting to cross. Al simply grinned: he had spent two happy hours staring at the water. George grunted and walked off and Keith then also grinned at me in friendly fashion although he was covered in sweat and oil from his unnecessary task.

I boarded the ferry, passing the Cap'n on his bridge. I had not had the opportunity of a word with Tinkess since I had seen him dancing towards me at the height of the crisis. Now as I stepped on board he turned to face me.

"Sorry Cap'n" I said. For a moment he simply kept his normally impassive face towards me, the drip in place as usual on the end of his nose. Then he raised his hand to remove his peaked uniform cap in a familiar gesture to allow him to scratch his head. The drooping eyelid of his right eye then drooped even more than usual as he replaced his cap and I realised that Cap'n Tinkess had winked at me. Then he turned to the wheel and I descended to my engine room.

Thoughtfully placed in the centre of my seat was the book, which Keith must have retrieved from behind the co-pilot's seat. The Cap'n rang the bell, I pressed the starter and worked the levers. We were off on another fourteen-minute routine run with twelve minutes 'average' reading time for me to get through.

Summer 1958 Canada

Wolves

The best way to see Canada, I was told, was to cross the country by train – a choice between the Canadian Pacific Railway (CPR) or the Canadian National Railway (CNR) when this was the accepted way to travel rather than by car or air. Luckily I had arranged a lecture tour and was to make the journey – Toronto to Vancouver in style, stopping off overnight in towns where I was scheduled to lecture and then picking up another train the next day. In Winnipeg I almost froze walking from the train to my hotel – the temperature was 40 degrees below freezing. In Prince Albert, sufficiently enveloped, as I thought, in a heavy coat I determined to take a short walk.

"Where are you going, Sir?" The doorman asked politely.

"Just a short stroll", I said airily.

"I wouldn't if I were you Sir and you haven't any glasses against snow blindness", he added encouragingly.

I thought he was putting on a show for the alien as foolhardily I stepped out into a cold I had not encountered before. Everything was crystal white. I crunched the snow underfoot while I absorbed the fact that no one else was walking or driving or to be seen. I managed to reach a bridge over a frozen branch of the Saskatchewan River by which time I was shivering uncontrollably. I just made it back to the hotel.

"You will need a hot drink now" said the doorman in proprietorial mode as he shook his head knowingly from side to side. The cold of January in Central Canada was a new weather experience for me. Then we came to the Rockies. The long train was weaving its way through the mountains and I sat at my window watching the last carriages enter a tunnel whose nearer end was disgorging the middle section of carriages before that too entered the next tunnel from which my carriage had just emerged. Then we passed through a tiny flat meadow like a secret garden in the mountains and there to my astonishment was a pack of wolves, perhaps 10 in all. They were playing, wrestling with one another in a carefree abandon, protected by the two biggest wolves that sat warily on the outside of the pack ready to warn of any danger. Not a single wolf so much as glanced at the train.

Canada January 1959

Canada by train

A month on the train from Toronto to Vancouver.

Waiter: "Did you enjoy your meal?"

"Yes"

"Wonderful Sir, thank you very much, you are welcome." The conductor came for a chat.

"I am surprised, with your English accent that a private (boarding) school has not snapped you up!" He said he was surprised so many immigrants from England did not stay in Canada.

"They all say wonderful, and then return home. The people here are rugged and good natured." Endlessly, we passed through the white smooth delicate beauty of the untouched snow.

"What do you think of Canada" became for me an all too frequent and sometimes embarrassing question, like a child asking for approval. I had two replies, depending upon my assessment of the speaker. The first: "Wonderful, has a great future." Or, more circumspectly, "Of course Canada is wonderful in many ways but it has its faults and failures like any other country." The trick was to assess my questioner correctly.

At Winnipeg I walked from the station to the Fort Gary Hotel – I would be sleeping there that night and then taking the train the following morning. In my room I received electric shocks – little ones – when I touched the light switches. It was then about 20 degrees below freezing. I was on a lecture tour to the Canada Clubs and my routine at each stop was the same. I would be met by a member of the Club committee who would take me to my hotel. Depending upon the time we would have lunch together then my host would leave me to my own devices until the evening when I would be taken to the hall where I was speaking. After delivering my lecture or talk I would be taken to a member's house for refreshment before returning to my hotel. There was little variation to this routine from town to town.

In those days lectures with slides were still a popular mode of entertainment. Canada still maintained archaic drinking laws which governed where and when you could have a drink. On one occasion my host came up to my room with me, went into the bathroom and found two tumblers and then took a flask from his hip pocket and poured two whiskies:

"To welcome you to Canada" he said genially. It was a dry hotel.

In Winnipeg, after my lecture, a woman came up to me to tell me she had come to Canada in 1913. She was from Hoxton and had proudly retained her cockney accent after all her years in Canada. She had never gone back to Britain. Meetings always began with a toast to the Queen – in water!

Many members of the Clubs had come out from England or Scotland: "I come from Liverpool." They had come to Canada as migrants either between the wars or in the aftermath of WWII.

Prohibition in America had seeped across the border into Canada and, for example, there were no bars in even some of the biggest hotels. There were, however, bottle openers fixed to the bathroom walls to assist those who indulged in a solitary bedroom drink. By drink here I mean whisky, There were bars for beer only, usually in hotel basements where you sat at a table – no standing allowed – while waiters circulated with trays of half pint size glasses of beer. There was always salt on the tables.

My host in Regina, a Scotsman from Fife, who had been in Canada teaching English for thirty years told me emphatically that there was no bar and no restaurant in Regina where you could obtain a drink. A high proportion of my audiences were former migrants from Britain and some of them complained that there was no outside interest in Canada and after years they still felt nostalgia for a Britain that they had left though they did not want to go back to it.

At Medicine Hat – 180 miles from Calgary, population 22,000 – I lectured first and then we had a sit down meal for all members. I was placed between two women at the high table. I asked the lady beside me to pass the butter.

She said: "I do like the way you say butter, Mr. Arnold. We have a prairie twang. My mother, you know, who came from England, always used to say to us children, say butter, but at school we picked up the prairie twang and wouldn't dare say butter there – they wouldn't have understood us. But we tried at home, but we lost it. But I love to hear it (the accent). I feel so conspicuous."

Memories of the old country. In a long distance bus: brilliant sun and blue sky allowing only tiny white clouds. A long straight road and to the side back from the road wheat elevators stood out stark like sentinels. In the far distance stretching to either side forever were the Rockies. Victoria, the Empress Hotel, the last bastion of a former generation of English immigrants. Tea time and a quartet playing Strauss for the old ladies in chokers. How do you like Canada?

The Canada Club(s) had a welcoming ceremony for new immigrant citizens. At a special party they would be welcomed into the community where they would meet the leading citizens. I was shown a list of new people to be welcomed at the next ceremony: two Finns, one Swede, two Germans, one Dutchman, four Chinese, one Russian and one Belgian. No Britons.

Back in Toronto I resumed my search for a job. I would be asked "How long have you been in Canada?" And then, "Never mind, you will feel better when you have been here longer."

Between searches and interviews I would go into one of the Fran's cafes, sit at the bar and have a piece of apple pie and a coffee. The Everly Brothers were top of the pops: You've got the whole world in your hands.

Canada 1958

An autumn lecture tour

I was scheduled to lecture in half a dozen towns along the dividing line between the provinces of Ontario and Quebec and since there were no great distances between the towns I found that I had most of the day to sightsee before giving an evening lecture. Or rather, my hosts would arrange a tour for me, for I was never given any free time. On one occasion two ladies drove me round the town pointing out its attractions.

"There are two churches – Roman Catholic and Presbyterian, which is your religion?"

"Neither" I said.

"Good. Then we can take you to see both of them." My education in this development region was to be extensive. Sherbrooke had a population of 65,000, its new university had 450 students, the leading school was the Bishop's College School and further off were farine (flour) mills to visit for the town served an important agricultural region. Meanwhile, arrangements had been made for me to visit in Shawinigan where there was a huge Alcan (aluminium) plant, a woollen mill and a Dupont plant. I was in the Alcan plant for an hour, most of the time being spent walking from one section to another, guided by a humourless supervisor who answered all my questions by reeling off statistics. The plants had a glorious setting of blazing Fall colours of the trees and turning leaves. A Mr. McNab showed me round his jumper factory that was situated in the township of Grandmere, population 15,000 of whom 300 made up his workforce. Grandmere also boasted a large paper mill, which, perforce, I visited. He explained that the population of the little town divided between the English speaking five per cent and the French speaking 95 per cent. He then took me to lunch in the Grandmere Inn. In the afternoon a Mr Pearson replaced Mr McNab and he took me round the Dupont plant where security was tight – I do not know what they made.

In both Canada and the States the concept of the organisation man had taken hold. All the executive staff sported identical red bow ties which were emphasised by the white of their coats. They looked harassed when Pearson, with me in tow, came into their sections. I commented upon the red bow ties and Pearson said they were worn to emphasise fire safety that week. Pearson never paused in describing the details of cellophane production but sometimes he got stuck.

"This is called an agitator" he said and at my raised eyebrow he said, "Well, that is what it does – agitates."

I was in an industrial growth centre of 42,000 population. DuPont, paper mills, a hydro centre, Alcan, woollens. By lecture time I felt equipped to give a talk on industrial Canada. I reached reception in the Arvida Alcan works at eight in the morning. The factory was shrouded in a thick fog. I was taken to my hotel and had breakfast while my guide had coffee.

The plant was one and a half miles long and employed 6,000 workers. It produced 330,000 tons of ingots in a year and these were first turned into strips and then wire. It was the largest such plant in the world I was informed with pride. It was an exciting plant and I became mesmerised by the process – ingots, strips, wires – which I observed for two hours! Most of the houses in the town were company built and then sold to the company's employees, 86.6 percent of whom owned their houses, probably one of the highest rates of company to employee sales in North America. A large dam had been constructed to provide the power for such plants. There were 12 turbines of 100,000 horsepower each. I think I visited all the communities in this productive area.

There were two dormitory towns – Jonquiere and Katogani – each with populations of 6,000, 18 schools and further educational statistics that suggested progress with a capital P. My last laid on visit was to a hospital, the third largest in Canada with 900 beds, a nursing school, 16 theatres and the use of colour TV for training purposes. Whatever I had learnt from this catalogue of visits was overshadowed by the last visit of all.

The final ward in the hospital was large and bright and contained 20 cots each occupied by a hydrocephalic child. They lay on their sides unable to move their huge heads, which anchored them to their mattresses with unblinking eyes staring at a world they could never belong to, waiting though this they did not know for death. One child especially caught my attention. His huge head was equivalent to five or more of the little body attached to it. His face occupied what, had he been upright, would have been the bottom of his huge head most of which was smooth without a feature or a wrinkle on it, like a giant white egg. The doctor seeing my attention said it would not live much longer. I wondered whether the child understood anything at all that took place round him. I cannot think of anything else in a long life that so moved me.

Canada 1960

ENGLAND 3

The Pennine Way

When I was 79 I finally decided to walk The Pennine Way. I had put it off for years because it was near, in England, and so had gone walking elsewhere instead but aged 79 I felt that time was running out. I took a train from London to Sheffield and then transferred to a small cross-country line from Sheffield to Manchester that passed through a number of small stops until at half way we came to Edale from whence the Pennine Way begins. Because I was travelling at the height of the season I had booked rooms in advance along the way and at Edale was to spend the night in the Rambler Inn, a new up market establishment for the rambling trade. In the afternoon I walked three miles to Jacobs ladder, the official starting point of the way, that led to the top of Kinder Scout mountain. That afternoon stroll was to get me in training. I returned to the Rambler Inn for my supper. The next morning, when I started, there were plenty of people, mainly day trippers, making the ascent up Jacobs ladder to the flat extensive stretch of bog at the top. I am a loner and have never gone on a walking expedition in company. As my guide book told me, "The Pennine Way is no longer routed over the fragile blanket bogs of the Kinder Scout plateau" but in order to avoid the crowd that had ascended to the starting point of the walk along the escarpment I cut across – as I thought – the bog plateau with the result that I spent an hour tiring myself unnecessarily before I escaped the bog and picked up the path I had wilfully bypassed. It was a clear day and the views were stunning. The walk along the escarpment was exhilarating but towards the end of the day, descending through woodland, I began to feel my age. During the sixteenth mile I slowed down to be passed by a group of three men in their forties who disappeared in the forest ahead. Almost collapsing from fatigue I needed a rest and had settled myself on the grass when the leader of the threesome that had passed me returned. He had seen how exhausted I was and had come back in case I needed help. He was without his backpack and now he carried mine to the top of the hill under the trees where the road crossed the Way. His companions were at the Snake Pass Hotel, a quarter of a mile away. His return and concern were part of the rambler camaraderie that distinguishes those who choose to walk the Pennine Way. I enjoyed a long cold beer in the Snake Pass hotel to help my recovery.

The Pennine Way 2011

A typical day on the Pennine Way

I had stayed overnight in Keld Lodge, in the village of the same name comprising a cluster of grey stone houses. Keld is the meeting place of the Pennine Way and the trans-Britain coast-to-coast way. The river Swale passes through Keld and has 'forces' (waterfalls) on either side of it. Sometimes, when on a big walk, I would search out the highlights mentioned in my guidebook but at others I would simply take in what I actually saw and only later find out what I had missed, although walking the length of the Pennine Way I found that I was becoming guidebook bound though in attempting to be too exact it could baffle: "Go through gate and wind down hill, then cross two fields, shut the gates behind you —. I left the Lodge at eight o'clock on a bright clear day that promised to be hot. I had a walk of four miles on a country road (apart from the Pennine Way) through a rising countryside of sharply outlined green hills that embraced a spectacular sill to reach the Tan Hill Inn at nine-thirty. The inn is England's highest pub at 1732 feet above sea level. There had been an earlier inn dating from 1586. The present inn dates from the 17th century. It is grey and built solid like a fortress to withstand the storms of winter. If you like solitude the inn would make a wonderful winter retreat, cut off by storms and snow. The inn was in business and I ordered a large coffee but to meet my request the barmaid brought me two coffees! The Tan Hill Inn marks the end of the Yorkshire Dales National Park and the beginning of the North Pennines area. The Inn stands on the edge of a great stretch of bleak and boggy moor in which it would be easy to get lost except for the white tipped marker posts. Sometimes the path across the moor was also revealed by flagstones that had been laid in especially difficult stretches of bog.

I took two hours crossing this stretch of moor – one of the bleakest I encountered. Then, gradually, the country changed and after crossing a bridge over a small river the path became easier and passed rare isolated farms though I met no one. A steady drizzle had replaced the morning sunlight. After an estimated 12 miles of walking a small mail van came towards me on it way to the remote farms. The driver stopped for a chat with me and told me I had another three miles to go to reach Bowes where I had booked a room in the Ancient Unicorn, a one time coaching inn. The pub I discovered did not open for business until six but after a wait a girl took me to my room and then brought me a pot of tea. After a shower and change of clothes I explored the town. Bowes has a 12th century castle built of stones from an earlier Roman fort. A drink, supper and then bed after what I thought of as an average day.

The Pennine Way 2011

Hadrian's Wall

Britannia was the northern province of the Roman Empire and Hadrian's Wall its most northerly military monument. It separated the Empire in its might to the south and acted as a barrier to the barbarians – Picts and Scots – to the north. The extension of Roman power in Britain can be traced through four sites: at Richborough, Porchester, Silchester, along stretches of the Pennine Way to York and then to Hadrian's Wall. Rutupiae (Richborough) became the gateway to the new

Roman Province of Britannia. The Claudian invasion occurred in 43AD and Rutupiae was the site where the initial camp for the invading army was constructed (the ditches remain). The Emperor Claudius spent 18 days in Britannia while the military conquest was carried out by Aulus Plautius. Originally intended as a supply base for the Roman army of 40,000, it almost at once came to be seen as the gateway to the new province and was occupied as such throughout the Roman period from 43AD to 410AD. The Portus Ruputiae was regarded as the entrance point to Britannia while the massive monumental arch acted as a symbol of Roman power. By the third century – 275AD, Ruputiae was to be rebuilt as one of the greatest Saxon Shore forts that guarded the coastline against the growing menace of the Saxons who regularly raided along the coast.

There are the remains of another major Saxon Shore defensive fort at Porchester. Medieval Porchester Castle was constructed in a corner of a huge Roman encampment that is surrounded by the most complete Roman wall in Europe north of the Alps, the walls standing almost to their full height around the fort.

Moving north to Silchester, which lies southwest of Reading, is the site of Calleva Attrebatun that was the nodal point of the road system to the south, the west and east and from which a major road went north. Traces of Roman roads have been detected at different points along the Pennine Way.

The Romans occupied the site of York in 71AD and the city was walled to become the most northerly military base in the Empire. Known as Eburacum it remained a garrison city until the final withdrawal of the Romans from Britannia in 400AD. The last monument to Roman power lay 100 miles to the north of York. Hadrian's Wall was built between 122AD and 128AD to act as part of Hadrian's defensive system circling the Roman Empire. The Wall begins at Wallsend east of Newcastle and stretches 84 miles to Carlisle. The most dramatic stretch of the wall runs along the escarpment that faces north in the centre of the country crossing the Pennine way.

The image of the lone legionary standing on the wall that divided the empire from the barbarians captured the imagination of the Victorians who saw the wall as a symbol of the far flung British Empire that was just reaching the apex of its power and worldwide spread. No other walk in Britain has the romantic appeal of Hadrian's wall.

England 2006

A disaster day

One of the absolute rules that I had observed in all my walking was to do it alone.

I am a loner by choice and used my walks to consider the multiplicity of subjects that engage me: philosophy and politics, art and poetry and always in the background the absurdities of the human condition. Besides, walking with other people means unwelcome adjustments since most of us have our own pace – too fast or too slow, talking or maintaining silence, when to stop for a rest or push on to gain distance. Walking alone I am at ease with myself.

Towards the end of my walk along the Pennine Way I broke my rule for the first time ever on a big walk. In my bed and breakfast the only other walker was Tony. He was walking the Pennine Way in stages - two or three stretches at a time – and had done the same walk as I had, having started earlier so that we did not meet one another on the way. We talked over breakfast and then set off together on what promised to be a hard day's walk. I cannot remember how, after all the years, I found myself walking with a companion.

The early part of the walk was through farm country and Tony kept checking every gate or field with his map. Eventually we got clear of the 'soft country' and began to rise steeply. We encountered a group of four: two men and two women whose average age I reckoned to be about 35 (I should have remembered that I was in the high seventies) and here I made the mistake of joining the group which meant keeping to their pace.

We climbed a steep stretch of mountain. Things always go wrong in clusters. It became bitterly cold and rain and sleet descended upon us. The foursome pushed on and I gave up trying to maintain their pace as they disappeared into the mist. I then had an attack of asthma even as I discovered that my windcheater which had been on all my trips for a quarter of a century had finally given up and the rain was seeping in and I was shivering with cold. Tony, about 30 yards ahead of me turned and made gestures to indicate a path. Sure enough when I reached him he was standing on a newly tarred road that was not shown on his map. I was freezing cold but the asthma had gone. Tony, who loved the new technology, now contacted the police in Dufton to inquire where this road went. There was a pause of 10 minutes while we waited for a reply – I now wanted to push on despite my disintegrating windcheater – when the police came on the air and said a rescue ambulance was on its way. Meanwhile, through breaks in the clouds we saw and heard a helicopter circling in an air search.

The ambulance arrived, followed by a saloon care with a middle-aged crew of man and woman and the team explained their procedure. They gave me a medical once over and found nothing wrong except that I was shivering with cold. I could have told them that but I suddenly felt that I owed them something. A helicopter, an ambulance and a private car all called into action for my benefit – a training exercise for the rescuers. Then the foursome who had ascended so bravely into the mist returned to say there was a raging storm up above. I meanwhile, had passed my medical and was handed over to the couple with the saloon car whose role was to take me down to Dufton. I and the efficient Tony had provided the occasion to have a practice rescue operation.

Back in Dufton at its premier inn I first had a beer and then found a bathroom in which I changed clothes before having a large and welcome lunch. Tony then appeared and had a beer with me. My walking plans for the day had been abandoned in dramatic circumstances which first annoyed me but then gave me pleasure as I and my plight had provided the occasion for a rescue drill that had clearly been carried out with commendable speed. I do not know what happened to the helicopter.

The Pennine Way 2011

BRITISH GUIANA 4

The Kaieteur Falls

Regarded as a wonder of nature, the Kaieteur Falls (a sheer drop of 741 feet) have gradually worked their way backwards to create a huge cavern that could house Salisbury Cathedral behind the curtain of water.

I had conceived the idea of forming a voluntary overseas service for young Canadians and was accompanied by two students (both Davids aged 18) who had just finished their grade 13 exams. A trip to British Guiana (still a British colony) was an experiment – we were to do some hard walking from village to village on the Rupununi plateau where I intended to collect folk stories from the Wapisiana Indians. The trip to the Falls was a final adventure before returning to Canada.

The Falls had to be approached by the Potaro River and this necessitated a boat. Mr Austen owned the only suitable craft for the river which included many rapids. He operated from Mahdia. From Georgetown I had made contact with Mr Austen and fixed a date to hire the boat and his services. A river steamer ran regularly from Georgetown to Bartica at the confluence of the Mazaruni and the Essequibo rivers. We boarded the steamer at 4.30am, found deck chairs and settled on the deck for the journey, which took about eight hours. The steamer was packed with passengers. We arrived at Bartica at 2pm but had further to go to Mahdia where Mr Austen would meet us and from where he operated his boat.

At Mahdia, as we manoeuvred alongside a crowded dock my attention was drawn to two waiting figures. Mr Austen – already described for me in

Georgetown – was unmistakable. A neat, dapper little man wearing a bowler hat and shirt collar and tie in Guiana's 80 degrees of humidity also sported a precisely furled umbrella. At the back of the crowded quay, leaning languidly against a wall, was a tall figure dressed in military tropical khaki shirt and shorts, wearing an unfashionable tropical topee and also, like Mr Austen, holding a tightly furled umbrella which he used as a walking stick.

Mr Austen identified me at once and introduced himself. We would have more travelling to do by lorry before we embarked in his river craft. He told me the British Army wanted the use of his boat since about 50 soldiers from Jamaica were assembling for a three-day jungle walk to the Falls. The army had not thought to hire the boat in advance – it was the only one operating on the Potaro - and they wanted to use it to drop off supplies along the river. Mr Austen, with a tinge of disdain in his voice at the failure of the army to think ahead, said that it was entirely up to me – there was enough space in his boat for an advance guard of soldiers with food to drop off at specified places. The boat was mine for the time I had booked.

At this point the languid young officer, Lt Hugh Keating, joined us:

"Mr Arnold?" he queried.

That evening over beer I did a deal with the Major and Lt Keating. They would augment my supplies with army rations and produce a small amount of money (much needed as my finances were running low); I would take the advance guard of 7 soldiers and supplies to be dropped off at two points along the river. The next morning we were up at 5.30am and met with the advance guard of soldiers while Mr Austen supervised where everything was stowed and where people should sit ("for balance" he kept saying). His wife and crew made another four people. Corporal Blaize, short, stocky, fair-haired with a ripe sense of cockney humour, clearly following instructions, insisted upon calling me 'professor' all the time.

It is exciting to go upstream in a fast flowing river that is frequently interrupted by rapids and Mr Austen, despite his bowler hat, knew how to handle his craft. We reached the beautiful Amatuk Falls at 11.30am and portaged round them before resting to eat our lunch. Eight miles further on we came to the Wanatuk Gorge which was enclosed by magnificent castle-like rocks. There was a small portage to do and we offloaded army supplies before we embarked upon the last stretch of river.

Mr Austen, I noticed, was a complete autocrat and his wife and crew jumped at his slightest command.

For the last few miles as we nosed our way upstream we could see the lip of the Kaieteur Falls and rising misty spray in front of them. There was a resthouse at the base of the path that led up to the top of the falls. We could stay in it but not the soldiers!

In the morning I paid Austen for we were booked to take the seaplane from the top of the Falls two days later. The next day, having first climbed to the lip of the Falls, we returned to the great pool at its base where the thunder of the fall meant we had to shout at one another to be heard and we swam across a turbulent pool to the rocks in the centre. We spent another day scrambling along the rock-strewn riverbed. On the third day we waited on a great flat rock by the lip of the Falls, until the seaplane arrived and took us back to civilisation. The pilot explained that when the plane took off and crossed the lip of the Falls we would feel a great upsurge of air which we did.

British Guiana September 1960

The Melvilles

The Rupununi plateau, covers about 40,000 square miles or a third of Guiana, and is one of the last open range regions in the world (or it was in the 1950s). It had been colonised or settled by the half Amerindian Melville family and of the 15 ranches on the Rupununi, all but two were owned by Melvilles. The first Melville was a Scotsman and a man of some education. He came to British Guiana (as it then was) in the 1890s intending to prospect for gold – the El Dorado of Raleigh's imagination – and diamonds. However, on a trip up the Essequibo river he succumbed to a fierce attack of malaria and his men left him for dead on a sand reef. He was found by Indians who nursed him back to health and thereafter he travelled and hunted with them until they settled in the Rupununi, a savannah country he came to love. He also adopted the Indian way of life. He took two wives and had ten children by them. He became the first serious cattle rancher on the savannah.

My landrover got stuck in a stream and we were unable to pull it out – it was then shortly after five in the late afternoon. We sent for help to the nearest ranch, which belonged to Charlie Melville, and he arrived at 8.30 on a tractor. We had met at Lethem on the border of the Rupununi. He had just returned to his ranch from Georgetown where he had been in police custody on a murder charge for killing a Brazilian although no evidence against him had been forthcoming and the charge had been dropped. After he had come with his tractor we had to wait until 11.30 while he sent for more fuel before the tractor winched us out of the stream. Charlie then said goodbye and went home and we continued on our way, picking up two girls who needed a lift. At two-thirty we reached Wichabai where Ted Melville, the eldest of the clan, had a large house. After he had got the story from us we settled in the bunkhouse by the airstrip.

We woke at eight to the sounds of a great storm that generated a strong and mercifully cool breeze that penetrated the upper floor of the bunkhouse where we had been sleeping. We were served with a splendid breakfast at a huge table that could seat his large family. We had fried eggs, lukewarm coffee, ham, butter, pancakes.

Ted Melville joined us for breakfast. He had married an Amerindian and had 13 children by her. At that time (1960) he had married a 19 year-old English girl who had come to Guiana for study purposes. Ted, who was then 59, had met her and they married. Her parents were on their way to the country from England! The house accommodated the large family of children, some still small, others in their teens or older. Melville grumbled that it was the school holidays and so they were overrun with children. The ranch house was raised high, a huge room of Berbice chairs, four Brazilian hammocks slung in the four corners of the room, partly partitioned off, and in the middle the enormous dining room table. A very handsome large framed photograph on the wall behind the head of the table was of old Melville, the father of the clam.

The Rupununi was running high as a result of the heavy rains. The Melvilles had their own kingdom here and did what they liked. A few years later they staged a revolt against the government in Georgetown although this changed nothing. At the village of Sand Creek I met a young Melville, John the son of Charlie, who was reading Lord Jim for his teacher's exam the following December. The government was looking at ways to bring development to the Rupununi though depending upon what sort of development was proposed, the government would have the Melvilles to deal with. The senior Melvilles were not impressed by the various missionaries who descended upon the country and in particular referred to the Born Again Christian Missionaries in the jungle of the deep south, who opposed anybody going into the area. These, they said, believed in segregated Christianity.

An Amerindian (Wapisiana) Story

A man and a woman, very happily married, lived together for a long time and then she died. The man was very sad and wept for now he was all alone. However, he had to go on doing his work; but now he had to prepare his own meals when he returned home. One day he left cassava in the house and when he returned he found it had been made into bread. He was greatly surprised because no one was there. Thereafter he would bring in food and when he returned again from fetching water, it would be cooked. This went on for some time and he was more and more surprised because no one appeared. Then one day he said aloud: "Who is it who is doing this for me?" And the woman who had returned to help him reappeared (made herself visible) and for a time they lived again as man and wife sharing their happiness. Then one day the woman was squeezing cassava and the matee – bag in which it is squeezed – burst, causing her to fall and hurt her hip. When this happened she said "Damn – is this what I returned for" and disappeared.

British Guiana 1960

Another Amerindian (Wapisiana) Story

Once, long ago, the Wapisiana men made a ladder of mud and climbed up into the sky to try to find god. When they did not find him they came back. They (a second time) took food with them but again did not find God. They returned to see their wives and then the ladder broke and they could not go up again. There were birds up there that they could hunt and they had liked the land there better than the Rupununi where they lived. There were nice things there, no work to do, no sickness. They met other people there who never worked. When they were hungry food came to them; they were friendly. They only needed one set of clothes for these never tore. There were also white people there, as big as the Wapisiana: they had long hair like women. They spoke a different language but the Wapisiana could understand it when they got there. This was heaven although they did not find god.

British Guiana 1960

Dadanawa Ranch

I was about to go up country in British Guiana to collect stories among the Wapisiana Indians who lived on the Rupununi plateau and my starting point would be the Dadanawa Ranch. At a typical colonial nuanced cocktail party in Georgetown I met Mr Turner – Harry – who managed the ranch. He said I should be welcome at Dadanawa although Mrs Turner, standing by somewhat the worse for wear from drink, weathered, and belligerent made plain that my descent upon her ranch would not be welcome. A lot of racism was apparent in Guiana, the 'Land of Six People', at that time and Mr Turner, waving an arm at the crowded room, said look at all these Negroes at this party but see what happens back in England – crimes, slums, rape. Our host was Tony Tasker, tall, elegant and clever who had been appointed (it was a political appointment) by the sugar company Bookers to modernise its attitudes towards Indians (the descendants of imported 'coolie' labour), and the black descendants of slaves as independence approached. Bookers was like a second government whose influence was to be seen everywhere and a joke that I heard frequently was that if you pulled the starter of an outboard motor it would splutter 'booker, booker, booker'. Mr Turner told me how much he admired Tasker who was doing a difficult political job with great aplomb. Elizabeth Tasker gave mixed race tea parties – an astonishingly late innovation for that country at that time. She had two tea services – one blue and one pink – and amused herself by putting pink cups on blue saucers and blue cups on pink saucers as an indication of what was to come. Mrs Turner said in indignant awe: "How can Elizabeth Tasker allow all those people to call her by her first name?" While Harry insisted he would welcome us at the ranch the attitude of Mrs Turner was more doubtful. She liked Bristol Cream sherry!

The ranch house was three quarters of a mile from the river, fenced and entered through a high gate with the name scrolled above it. There were half a dozen buildings painted white, the bunkhouse, the guesthouse, a windmill, the hands' house and the Turners' house. The ranch worked 2,500 square miles of the Rupununi and carried 25,000 head of cattle. In those days the Colonial Office was pursuing development in a last burst of paternalism before independence and in Georgetown there had been talk of trade unions being established. This was cause of high amusement among the ranchers – there were fifteen smaller ranches in the hands of the ubiquitous Melville family – who would introduce them? The

Indians wouldn't organise them and the ranchers were solid in their opposition.

The European members of the ranch would have made an ideal cast for an American cowboy film. They were all characters in their way and had got in the habit of playing their parts. Stan Brock stood out. He was English, 25 years old with a slight beard and side burns, long hair, wearing a wide-brimmed hat, tight jeans and barefooted until he got out on the range. As Mr Turner told me Brock had come to the ranch when he was seventeen, had picked a fight with every vaquero in turn and beaten them, had learnt to do everything on the ranch better than anyone else whether horse breaking, fighting, or drinking. He must have read some cowboy stories before he came to Dadanawa. Mr Turner clearly relied upon him. He took me to watch the castration of a stallion, which was already tied down by the Indians but Stan checked the ropes first, gave it an injection and then operated. When he discovered that I had written a book about my travels in Borneo, Brock confided that he was half way through writing a book about big game in South America and wanted to know what market there would be for such a book in Britain. Later he told me his ambition was to shoot the big five in Africa, which I subsequently learnt he did and wrote about it.

We would meet on the veranda for drinks before a meal and the Turners would dominate the conversation with their anecdotes about the government in Georgetown. Developers seemed to think that the Rupununi was an ideal area for development and it would be visited by "experts" to decide how it could be used. Vincent Harlow (I had attended his lectures at Oxford) and the socialist Rita Hinden had made recommendations as did others but Cheddi Jagan's wife Janet on a visit pointed out that the grass was so sparse that probably the best use for the Rupununi was as a cattle range, which was what it was already, but since she was an American and a communist no one took any notice of her advice.

I had arrived at Dadanawa in time for lunch and we made up an interesting table between us: the Turners, our hosts,

Stan Brock, Jimmy Brown, an old rough Scot who had become a fixture and young George Seers, a red-haired country lad who had come to Dadanawa straight from finishing his national service. He had only been there for ten days, Turner told me, and Brock was breaking him in, three days on a horse until he could hardly stand. He said little at lunch and was almost asleep in his place. At least Mrs Turner liked the veranda where she held forth – She did not like being in a cage she told me. She grumbled because she had not expected anyone for lunch. Stan Brock, enjoying his food and drink, said to me: "You will find the centre very comfortable" as opposed to the discomfort and cabouri flies that I would have to cope with once I began walking. Turner disliked the missionaries and derided the government for its development policies. He was against democracy – "A man who can read and do something is privileged" he said, "a white face is also a privilege", a comment that was both shrewd and near the knuckle. As he held forth – the representative of a dying breed throughout the empire – Mrs Turner nodded and interposed vigorous agreement with what he said. Brock nodded agreement but clearly had heard all Harry's reservations about progress many times. Jimmy Brown said the labourer was worthy his hire and he was content with his position (whatever that was).

I came to like Mrs Turner despite her pleasure in acting as a tartar to frighten her guests. What she needed was flattery but she didn't get much of it on a working ranch. In the late afternoon, after a shower, I took a carefully hoarded bottle of Bristol Cream (I had sought advice in Georgetown) to a delighted Mrs Turner who at once took me round her garden where she husbanded oranges, grapefruit, bananas, vegetables and orchids. Dinner consisted of soup with a hot pepper wine added, lamb chops, fruit and yoghurt and coffee. Mrs Turner retired at once after the meal while the rest of us only lingered briefly though Harry insisted upon drinking a nightcap with me.

British Guiana 1960

Maurice Nascimento

Maurice Nascimento was blessed with a thin head, alert and probing eyes and the capacity to maintain a one-sided conversation indefinitely. The British colony of Guiana had been his birthplace and was his home and, as he told me, he had been in and out of the bush all his life. He had an odd habit of ending every sentence or phrase with a sort of strangled ugh as though to dismiss whatever he had just said before proceeding with his next anecdote or tale. No one else in a country where everyone had an opinion could match him in the quality and range of his stories. At the end of our trip he would fly us off the river above Kaieteur Falls in a seaplane. He described the effect of being bitten by the caburi fly for which the Guianese bush is notorious. As he told us solemnly, you get bitten by the caburi fly for 12 hours of daylight and then by mosquitoes for twelve hours of dark ugh. He took a package from a belt pocket – it was part of his raconteur stock in trade equipment – to show us gold nuggets, cut diamonds "beauties" ugh "so I must avoid being knocked down at night!" He claimed to know most of the interior except, curiously" where we were intending to go.

I met him again in the Club where he promptly requisitioned me as a willing audience for his stories. He possessed an extraordinary store of information. As he got underway I determined simply to follow his free flow and hope to retain it for future reference. This was possible but difficult since, once underway, he never stopped. He was contemptuous of the missionaries who went to the extreme south of the country in the jungle that merged into that of Brazil:

"The Wai Wai should be left alone" he insisted.

Guiana had been described as the "land of six people". This he said was true and therefore the Colonial Office did not like it, from which remark I inferred he was anti-the activities of that body which he said was hindering the move towards independence. From the Colonial Office he jumped to education that had to be taken at its extremes.

"I have lived close to the ground" he said "and am happy in the bush" ugh "but I also like the Ritz from time to time".

He liked visiting all the art museums of Europe. He said how he had told Americans visiting Guiana, "Don't give me your standard of living, I like my own." He had liked America until 1958 when he went there and found that 99 per cent of the people did not own anything.

He switched, as he did most of the time, to another subject. Guiana was not yet a country. When he was asked to fill in a form, which included space for RACE – he put 'Human Race'. An international ring controlled the diamond industry and included Jews. In Kenya Williamson had to sell out to the Syndicate, they would murder him if necessary, if there was no other way to gain control. Once, in London he had gone with his sister to look at the Crown Jewels that he dismissed as not very good. In his bachelor bungalow he had a collection of blowpipes, curare arrows and bows and arrows.

His stories were clichés but coming at you like machine gun bullets they kept the listener wide awake. He was a Catholic and regarded the five great encyclicals as his Bible. He had become interested in books when he found a friend telling him things about the jungle although he knew the man had never been there. As a result he obtained original copies of Brown – the 19th century English explorer – and Schomberg. He wanted the different races to keep their traditions and not be melted into a Guiana pot. BG, he said, had no background while he had great admiration for the English with 1000 years of background behind them. In Portugal, which he had recently visited, two out of five palure Inglese (spoke English). The English had bought up the Madeira and Port.

He was crazy about Kaieteur, he had flown all over it and was probably the only man to have bathed in the pool at the foot of the falls. We swam in the pool later. British colonial civil servants were dedicated. (There was no consistency in his judgements). It was businessmen who had spoilt the colonies.

An American had said to him, "Look at all these arrogant Germans here" to which he had riposted, "What of all these arrogant Americans."

When he is in Europe and in a hotel he says, "I am poor, from an underdeveloped country – don't charge me, but they do!"

There is a colour bar here in Guiana but people behave in their traditional manner and do not realise that they are part of it. For a full life must do both extremes – he earned $20,000 in a good year diamond mining. He told us the legend of the old man of Kaieteur. He was in a canoe eating his lunch ugh and went over the edge and now at the bottom is a stone shaped like an upturned canoe. He laughed at the efforts of an official of Demba (the bauxite company), a personnel manager who wanted to teach him how to live with the people.

At the end of the evening – I wanted to write up my notes to cover this flood of information, counsel, anecdote and wonderful prejudices – he came up with jungle advice: if three men are walking along a jungle path in single file beware of snakes. The first man will disturb a sleeping snake and then pass on, the second man will anger the snake, the third man will get bitten.

British Guiana 1960

BORNEO

5

The Plieran River

A fierce and beautiful tributary of the mighty Rejang, the river cut its way through the jungle so that it flowed or rushed between high banks while the jungle treetops spread a canopy over it. The river's source was on the divide between Sarawak and Kalimantan and as it dropped from the central plateau to the Rejang Valley it passed alternately through narrow gorges where great rocks like sentinels almost meeting mid stream reduced its width to 10 yards of roaring water until it levelled in a smooth stretch where it might be as much as fifty yards wide and flow for as much as 200 yards before dropping though another gorge.

The jungle teemed with game and on one day alone we encountered red deer, barking deer, wild pig, gibbons and where the sun penetrated the treetops to light up sandbanks monitor lizards basking upon them. The absence of human beings had made the game tame and unwary. And that absence made it a jungle paradise.

One day in the late afternoon we came to a huge lake where the river had widened over a level area. We beached our canoe to make camp for the night and across half a mile of water saw that the trees on the other shore were black with peculiar birds. It was the resting place of the great fruit bat and as the dusk turned to night they took off making their strange cries in search of the mangosteens and lychees that abounded here.

Once, in the early morning, standing by a side stream that fed into the river I found myself staring at a magnificent brown civet cat with a pointed white snout and a long white-tipped tail stretched out straight behind it, before he trotted past me, head up, sniffing but otherwise ignoring my presence.

The further upstream we went the more difficult it was to travel on the water because of the succession of gorges where we would have had to haul the canoe. So we took to the jungle, walking alongside the river where that was possible or making land detours. My guide was Madang, a Sebop from the Tinjar, who had been here before searching for the tracks and pathways used by the Indonesians when they crossed the border.

On one evening I went hunting with Madang. We spotted a honey bear – they stand at three feet – and Madang fired at it though he should not have done so for it is a protected species – but the bear ambled away into the undergrowth.

Once when I was alone by the river I heard a crashing through the undergrowth above me and a magnificently-antlered deer came down to the brink of the steep bank on its way for water. Without thinking I raised my gun and fired and the deer leapt into the air with a cry before tumbling down the near vertical bank to collapse at my feet. It lay there, one beautiful eye looking its reproach at me before it gave a great shudder and was dead. That reproachful eye remained in my mind for years and persuaded me never to shoot game again, anywhere.

On one occasion Madang and I came through the jungle to an opening in the trees where we could sit at the top of the bank and watch the river below us. At that point it was about forty yards wide, swift flowing but smooth. Opposite us was what looked like a mud slide sheer from the top of the bank to the riverside. I was about to ask Madang what had caused it when he whispered, "keep very still". Then I heard a great chittering as a school of otters came along the path they had made at the edge of the river bank to follow one another in quick succession down the mud slide into the water. Led by a big male otter they fanned out across the river and were carried downstream about 100 yards before they clambered out of the water and repeated their circuit – along the path, down the slide, down the river and out for another go. Their excited chittering was the nearest I could imagine to otter laughter. They must have made this circuit about eight times, the big otter always in the lead with its head stretched up and eyes alert when I moved my head only slightly but that was enough of a threat and the big otter gave a sharp warning cry and a dozen otter heads at once submerged out of sight.

Sarawak (Borneo) 1955

Walking in the Jungle

Not just walking in the jungle but creating a path from a Longhouse to a river junction and encouraging sixty porters carrying supplies to sustain a base camp where an airdrop of supplies would be made later.

Our party began this journey in seventeen canoes, two or three men to each of them, to take us about a mile along the river before the point where we began walking overland. The men shouted farewells to the people of the Longhouse who watched our departure and the canoes spread out across the river like a straggling armada, the weaker soon falling behind, while the rain came down to drench everyone.

The narrowing river twisted and turned, overhanging trees reached farther and farther across it, and kingfishers shot dazzling blue over the water. When we reached the point where we would leave the canoes the porters cut staves to aid their walking and readjusted their loads. I paid off the canoes and then we began the jungle trek to the Plieran.

A Kayan who knew the way took the lead and the porters plodded along in single file, at an even pace, their bodies slightly bent forwards to ease the strain of their loads. The jungle was thick and a great deal of cutting had to be done. Every forty minutes we halted to await the stragglers who arrived when the leaders were ready to start walking again. The river wound between high forested banks and shafts of sunlight came through the trees to make the tumbling waters sparkle while the leaves, still wet from the rain glistened. We kept going until three thirty in the afternoon when we found a convenient open space beside the river and made camp.

Relieved that the day's carrying was over – this was to be a short day – the porters sat by their loads rolling their strong tobacco in dry leaf to make loose, fat ended cheroots and scraping the clusters of slug like leeches off their bloodied ankles while we waited for the stragglers. Then the headman, Taman Bulan, in the role I soon discovered he enjoyed most, issued orders and the men dispersed to find the materials needed to make a covered camp.

Every man, as a matter of course, carried a parang or machete that was an essential tool for jungle travel. The Kayans handle their parangs, which they keep dangerously sharp, with great dexterity; green saplings and trees were cut down and trimmed with astonishing speed, while the older men collected rotan creeper, sometimes as much as 200 feet long, which is one of their most important natural resources. Within an hour the whole camp structure was completed, just giving standing room at the front, but with the roof sloping steeply backwards to within two feet of the ground to allow the rain to run off. There was enough floor space for two feet per man so that at night they were close packed in a row. That first day's travel, though short, was typical of a routine we fell into.

As soon as it was light – just after six o'clock – we cooked rice, packed, and the porters prepared their loads for the day. As soon as we had eaten we began our walk which would last from seven thirty to about half past three in the afternoon, sometimes through fairly easy country, though more often than not two men in the lead were cutting a path through thick primary jungle, taking fifteen or twenty minutes to negotiate a difficult patch.

This particular walk occupied four days but the routine was repeated whenever we had to move from one camp to another. The obstacles were always the same: rain, insects, leeches, crossing and re-crossing small rivers that overnight had become torrents as they received the rain from their headwaters.

Sarawak (Borneo) 1955

SPAIN

6

The Pilgrim Way

In 1993 I spent months in Spain following in the footsteps of George Borrow whose book The Bible in Spain had been a best seller in the 1840s. By accident, I found myself on the Pilgrim Way to Santiago de Compostello:

I left Astorga and had just completed the first kilometre and was settling into my stride when there came towards me on a bicycle one of those large comfortable friendly women who spend their lives helping other people, whether asked to do so or not. She wobbled to a stop as she beamed a greeting:

"Buenas Dias, peligro?"

"Si, si" I nodded, "soy peligro."

She was an organiser, I could tell even before she began to give me instructions. "But you are on the wrong road, Senor, this is not the pilgrim's way."

"It is my way," I replied firmly. "I am going to Bembibre."

"But are you not going to Santiago like all the others?"

"Yes, I am going to Santiago as well, but not like all the others. I take a tortuous path." This Jesuitical comment of mine was not well received.

Slightly flustered but determined to do her good deed for the day she became stern: "But the path is back there," and she pointed behind me. "You are going the wrong way."

"Senora, Bembibre lies ahead of me," and I pointed behind her but she only shook her head with irritation.

"The pilgrim way lies over there," she repeated,

now spacing her words slowly in case the foreigner was not understanding properly, "and you must take it in order to be a proper pilgrim."

"I know," I replied "but I want to go this way. I saw where all the other pilgrims went," I added mendaciously, "and besides, I am not a proper pilgrim."

She ignored this odd statement of mine, perhaps she did not understand what I meant, and continued: "But you do not understand: a peligro has to go along the path."

"But I am a different sort of peligro, I am walking all the way to Cape Finisterre," I exaggerated for I have always found that a little exaggeration does wonders for an argument. Exasperated and angry with me because her intended help had been rebuffed she let out a long sighing "oooh" and shrugged a dismissal as she heaved herself back onto her bicycle and continued on her way. She did not deign to answer my "Gracias, Senora", which made me feel I had been mean not to surrender to her good intentions.

Summer 1993 Spain

The Bible in Spain

I once spent months in Spain following in the footsteps of George Borrow whose book The Bible in Spain, *published in 1842, was a best seller.*

When he was in Toledo Borrow stayed at the Posada de los Caballeros (the inn of the gentlemen), which he describes in flattering terms. It is one of the very few inns he actually names and I had hoped to locate it but the tourist office had not heard of it and no such inn was listed, so I assumed that time and decay had taken care of it.

At the end of a day's exploration I came up a series of steps and then a steep incline to enter a small square where half a dozen tables had been arranged outside a bar. I was in need of refreshment and selected a table that faced down the length of the little square. A woman of severe if striking features rose from the only table that was occupied and came to serve me.

I ordered a glass of wine and relaxed. The sun came out after a day of rain and with it the people so that soon all the tables were occupied.

The woman who I assumed was the hostess had to leave her friends and take up her position inside the bar, handing drinks through a hatchway to a small belligerent man who now waited upon the tables. I was still learning Spanish customs and though I had often been served tapas – snacks of olives, nuts or some other savoury trifle that came with the drink – I was not sure whether the tapa was automatic (paid for, as it were, by the drink) or an optional extra at the discretion of the host. The newcomers who had arrived after me had all received a dish of nuts with their drinks; I ordered a second glass of wine and noticed how, when he collected it from the hostess at the window, she pointed to a dish of nuts and then gestured towards me. Her meaning was obvious enough and she was atoning for her failure to give me tapas in the first place but the man shook his head and only brought me the glass of wine. I accepted this slight without comment but, since everyone else had been given tapas automatically, became increasingly irritated. By this time I had drunk two glasses of wine sans nuts, and felt I deserved better treatment. I beckoned the small belligerent man, I think he was the proprietor and husband of the striking looking woman who was more than a head taller than he, and ordered a third glass of wine.

I was now feeling as angry as Borrow did whenever he believed the English were being slighted. The little belligerent man duly returned with my third glass of wine but still no tapas. I, meanwhile, had looked up nuts in my pocket dictionary and asked him: "Senor, why do you not also give me a dish of nuts (tuercas)?" and I waved a casual hand at the other tables. He, however, regarded me with astonishment, as well he might, and shrugged.

"Tuercas", I repeated and he remained before my table as though I had gone mad. Of course I had looked up the wrong nut and was fiercely demanding the kind which accompanies a bolt. I returned to my dictionary, rectified my absurd though understandable linguistic error, and then demanded a dish of peanuts (cacahuetes). Enlightenment suffused his grumpy face to be followed by a big delighted smile at my stupidity; he went to his wife, told her of our passage of misunderstanding with evident pleasure and then, in compensation for his past bad behaviour, brought me an enormous dish of nuts which he placed before me with elaborate courtesy, for there were certain depths to my host.

As he placed the nuts on the table in front of me I happened to look over my shoulder and saw on the wall above my head a plaque with the name of the small square: La Plaza Santiago de los Caballeros. Astonished at the coincidence, I asked my belligerent friend whether there had ever been a posada of that name in the square. Now it was his turn to be astonished.

"Of course, Senor, it was famous, at the end of the square," and he pointed to the far end from where I was sitting. "but it was demolished a long time ago." He was intrigued at my question and his former unfriendly belligerence now gave way to frank curiosity:

"But how did you know about an inn here?"

I shrugged, a small revenge: "An ancestor of mine stayed there 150 years ago," I replied with suitable hauteur.

Back at his window he talked to his partner with lively animation that put his earlier surly behaviour to shame.

Spain 1993

Lost in Valladolid

I got lost in the centre of Valladolid as I searched for the English School so sought directions. There were lots of people hurrying past to choose from for it was midday, but a kind of inborn perversity led me to select a middle-aged woman whose robust physique, big bosom and severe features would generally earn her the description of "forbidding".

"Por favor, Senora… I began, but with a sweeping gesture she said "I do not speak to strangers."

"But madam, I am lost."

"Senor, I repeat, I do not speak to strangers."

"But I am not a stranger, I am only lost."

"What do you mean, not a stranger! I have never seen you before."

"That does not make me a stranger, madam."

"Then what, may I ask, are you?"

"I am an Englishman."

"You are English?" She invested her voice with astonishment: "The English are all by the seaside." This was an appropriate rendering of her contempt for a people who only went through her country to sunbathe on the Costa Brava or Costa del Sol. She looked at me with new interest: "You are English, you say?"

"That is so madam and I seek your help."

She stood like a battleship temporarily becalmed but getting up fresh power: "How may I be of assistance?" she asked, the earlier suspicion in her voice now tempered with a softer note of helpful inquiry. I gave her the address of the English School.

"The English School!"

She had not heard of it, so I enlightened her: "It was established in the reign of your King Philip II, in 1590," I said and added, for good measure: "We used to come here for other reasons in those days, not just the sea."

And then she smiled and gave me precise directions.

Spain 1993

Carmona

Carmona is a film-set of a town whose narrow streets of white painted houses twist into small squares while great studded doors guard the ancient palaces of nobles. I only saw one of these doors open, and since a man and woman were entering I made the mistake of a typical tourist and went to follow them, assuming that one palace at least was on show to an inquiring public, but the woman turned to murmur that it was their home. The town appears largely untouched by time except for cars and tourists, and with regard to these latter it clearly only encourages the upper end of the trade for it boasts one five-star hotel, one four-star hotel and a parador.

I wanted to find out the times of buses to Cordoba in the morning and was directed back to the bar where I had alighted earlier in the day. The clientele of that bar was made up exclusively of old men: a celebration of some kind was in progress and everyone was drinking brandy. Behind the bar, perched on a high stool, was a fat girl staring with rapt attention at the corner above her head where King Kong flickered back and forth across the screen. I approached the bar opposite the girl and inquired, politely I hoped, but raising my voice to make myself heard above the general din, the times of buses to Cordoba in the morning. I felt half ashamed at breaking in upon such concentration. I need not have worried. There was no answer, no movement, no indication that she had heard me. I tried again, my voice a decibel sharper. The same negative result. I tried a third time. Still no response. A freshly opened bottle of brandy was now coming along the bar, one old man at a time, and the nearest ancient sitting up to the bar next to the space I had occupied gave me a careful look; he had, I believe, been trying to decide whether I was German, American, Scandinavian or Italian and now he went into action on my behalf. He leant forward and rapped sharply with his knuckles on the bar beneath the fat girl's nose. Startled away from King Kong she looked round.

"This Caballero" – and he indicated me with a polite flourish – "requires your attention." Once more I put my question and, after some disentangling, discovered that the Cordoba bus went at eight thirty in the morning. By this time the brandy bottle had reached the old man beside me: first he filled his own glass; then he stretched over the bar and brought back a clean glass which he placed in front of me and filled to the brim with brandy.

Gratefully I toasted him: "Salud – but I am English," I said and he gave a slow smile in delighted acknowledgement that I had guessed correctly his failure to place my nationality.

Spain 1993

TURKEY

Jerusalem to Istanbul

Spent the night in a tiny Arab hotel – a narrow bed in each of four corners with a small table beside it with a glass of water for the night – very hot and perspired – mosquitoes – in the morning I counted the fifteen huge bed bugs I had collected during the night and dumped in my water so they formed a scum on its surface – on leaving, our host on guard at the door of his lodging house told me he would assist us – very cheaply – to cross the border into Jordan – took a bus to Haifa – 'J' now seemed willing to come with us – money had arrived from London and so paid for our cheap tickets on the Marmara (Haifa to Istanbul in five days) – only just in time, bought melons for food on the way, no spare cash for luxuries – as the steamer nosed its way out of the port Haifa looked fine as it extended up the hillside but I only experienced a sense of enormous relief to be out of Israel – we each had a card describing ourselves spuriously as members of the Australasian Press – 'A' went to see the Captain to explain that we were experimenting – how far we could travel with very little money – He did not believe her but she had enormous persuasive charm so he gave us the run of the ship (but no food) – after the wealthy ones had eaten I would go round the dining saloon and collect the uneaten bread rolls – 'J' and I slept on deck that night in the prow of the ship

The next day we arrived at Alexandretta as it was then still called – Iskendrun today – the Marmara was to be in port for the afternoon – the waterfront was yellow and glistening – we went ashore – hills rose up behind the dusty town which had every kind of shop from sweets and toys to carpets – we were greeted repeatedly though the police were suspicious of our 'for Israel only' passports – many of the men wore traditional pantaloons, some rode donkeys – a little band of three went slowly round the market place – two men with drums which they beat steadily (the saz) and a third who alternated with first a reedy flute and then a silver trumpet. The Muezzin was called from the minaret of the mosque that commanded the square – it was the first time I had heard the call to prayers – shoe shine boys seeking work were defeated by our sandals – through a great market shed we found an Arab restaurant where a man performed a solo orgasmic dance.

Mersin at eight in the morning – 'J' now feeling free insisted that we took a bus to Tarsus to see the birthplace of St Paul – a sudden conversion to Christianity – we only have two hours I reminded him but he dug his heels in so, accompanied by an unwilling Turk who spoke English and had befriended us, we took a ramshackle bus to Tarsus – Alexander the Great in the early days of empire building had come south through the Cilician Gates on to Tarsus and then down the coast until he reached Tyre and commenced the bloodiest of all his sieges – the only thing to see in Tarsus was a Roman Arch of the second class – a bus for Mersin came at last but I knew we would be late and as it topped a ridge from which one could look down on the sea we saw the Marmara already a mile off shore and steaming away with our meagre belongings on board. We had a conference – our Turkish friend, now convinced we were mad, insisted the two women could not hitch hike – not to be recommended at any time but it was now Ramadan – and volunteered to pay their air fares to Adana – 'J' and I to hitchhike – Turkey at this time had not been opened up to tourists.

A lift on a huge truck piled high with bales of sheepskins – four soldiers already on the bales which swayed perilously when we took a corner – we were four metres above the ground – bitter cold – could look down the mountain pass and see the headlights of other great trucks grinding their way through the Taurus Mountains below us – tried to sleep but

JERUSALEM TO ISTANBUL

feared rolling off so sat hunched to look down the pass – a brilliant moon revealed grim, awe-inspiring mountain peaks – stopped at teahouse – the truck to rest until dawn – it was 2am – other trucks also came to rest here, where the highway split, one road to Konya, the other to Ankara. We were invited to take shelter in tent with rough roadside Turks – no more traffic till dawn, which shimmered brilliant across the mountains. Wonderful green valley of trees – walking between lifts – striated green hills and then rising behind them gaunt black rock peaks – through villages where the dogs came out to snarl at us – early to work Turks in little pony-drawn traps – a lift to Nigde village – road gradually descending to the plain – two way conversation with Turks in a lorry – neither understood the other but that did not matter – lorry left us and we washed in the village stream – had tea and bread in an early morning eating house – a student followed us, he wanted to speak French – he took us to see the village of Bor off the main highway – mud walls and bushes overhanging them – the houses were two-storied, upper windows boxed outwards – he led us through the village where we were inspected – he took us to his home and his room was a typical student's – we discussed his course – he took us to an orchard and we ate apples and apricots. He insisted we went back to his house – small boy brought in a huge round tray covered with meat and salad and Arab bread and fruit – after this unexpected luxury meal he walked with us to the petrol station on the highway where he said we would get a lift. He left us with regret – a Syrian who had just filled up his petrol tank said he would give us a lift – he was going to Ankara – and then changed his mind – two to one and we looked a disreputable pair despite washing in the stream – the Anatolian Plain – little villages – one on a steep hill – a horseman came racing past, a bandolier over one shoulder, a rifle over the other – tiny rest house gave us a bed each for the night for one Turkish pound – in teahouse where the locals questioned us about our journey – it is surprising how you can get by with a little German, occasional French, some English and signs – after telling our life stories our interrogator said: "I think you are short of money" to which we nodded.

"Would you like 20 pounds?"

We nodded out of curiosity.

"We" and he included the others in a gesture "will give you 20 pounds if you promise to walk through Greece with a placard on your backs that says: Cyprus for the Turks" – we didn't nod.

Ankara large and expanding – many new buildings – found two pumps in the centre of the old town – a stranger came to talk and appeared delighted to find we were English and not American - invited to his flat – beer, cigarettes, sweets – his sons came in to talk with us – a social occasion – our host directed us to a small hotel whose receptionist was an American – too expensive – tea and then wended our way through back streets to a smaller hotel – a pound each – Turks delighted with our patronage.

The glittering skyline of Istanbul – 44 mosques grace it – is dominated by the Aya Sofia (Emperor Justinian's masterpiece to represent the Divine Wisdom) – the Blue Mosque graced by its six elegant minarets – and the vast Suleymaniye Mosque – each emphasizing the timelessness of this many layered city which was already great two thousand years ago– we imbibed all this later – but Istanbul is also possessed of an essential seediness which adds to its grandeur. Hitchhiking on empty stomachs can exhaust and that first night, from midnight to dawn we exhausted ourselves still more by traversing, crossing and recrossing our steps in the dark. In tiny alleyways the rats would emerge to sort out the garbage, rats that had grown huge on the largesse of the city. Sudden shrieks of rage announced territorial confrontations of cats – Istanbul is a city of cats – before they set out in search of rats. The moon was up, its soft yet sharp light casting shadows – cats or rats would scurry across alleyways as we entered them and sudden squeals announced the death of a rat. Down to the waterfront of the Golden Horn whose sullen waters lapped the shoreline – across on the other side the Galata skyline was dominated by the Galata Tower – we climbed to it in a silence zone and through out the night met no one. As dawn broke we found our hotel and slept through the day.

Israel and Turkey 1957

Dogs

I came round the steep shoulder of the hill to see a sight I shall never forget. Perhaps 200 yards ahead of me and down the slope of the hill was a huge flock of sheep tightly gathered round a solitary tree. I had heard their bells for some time before I caught sight of them without realising what the sound meant. Standing under the tree leaning on a great stick was the shepherd, while a boy on a donkey circled the flock. Beyond the sheep the hill sloped ever more steeply to the valley far below where trees marked the course of a river. It was an idyllic, Biblical scene of a kind that could hardly have changed in centuries.

I continued towards the flock enjoying the serenity of this ancient rural picture when seven of the largest sheep detached themselves from the rest and came racing towards me, baying in that deep-throated way which belongs to only the most savage of dogs, and this indeed was what they were. I had forgotten about dogs. These were massive Anatolian shepherd dogs. They were huge with particularly powerful thick shoulders. They wore wide iron collars with two inch iron spikes sticking out of them, which perform a dual task; they make it impossible for the dog ever to lay its head flat on the ground to rest, so that they are always watchful with savage tempers to match; and in a fight with wolves the spikes, like a weapon, will make the dogs even more formidable than nature and sleeplessness have rendered them already.

I stood still, having no weapon. The dogs reached the road and, trained in attack, formed a half-circle round me, growling and snapping. Turning slowly from side to side and saying 'hus, hus' as though I was used to such creatures, I watched in awed and terrified horror at their large blackened teeth, which their drawn-back muzzles now revealed. Saliva dripped from their mouths and my apparent unconcern did nothing to quieten them.

The shepherd had forced his way through the flock scattering sheep as he came running up the hill towards me; the boy on the donkey was banging his heels into its flanks, forcing it with shrill cries at an unwonted speed up the hillside. I just hoped they would reach me, or rather their dogs, in time. The dogs were now closing in, the nearest no more than three yards from me, and I knew that once one made a dash for a bite they would all follow. I thought of Orestes in antiquity torn to pieces by wild dogs – the thought gave me no comfort.

I gave an extra hard stamp with my foot just as the largest and most savage-looking dog moved a pace nearer. The gesture worked, for it backed off snarling and then the shepherd arrived and, not without effort drove his dogs back. The boy leaped off his donkey and, swishing a cane, also drove them back. Neither of my rescuers took any notice of me whatsoever and though they were now under their control the dogs continued snarling furiously no more than ten yards behind me as I resumed my walk. I have rarely been so frightened in my life.

Summer 1986 Turkey

I am pleased to meet you

In a bar for a drink – lugubrious barman wanted to talk or rather to find out all he could about me.

"Where was I from, what was I doing in Turkey, where had I been so far, what did I think of Turkey, what did I do for a living? When explaining my journey I found that my map was an infallible aid to such one-sided conversations. I could point out where I had been and where I was going. The barman invited two other men to join us and question me. One of them, the barman said proudly, was a teacher, as though this would enable him the better to fathom what I was doing though he had no more German or French than did the others so our conversation remained limited.

Later in a tea garden I made the mistake of giving an inquisitive young man one of my panatella cigars. He came back to me later to ask for another – he said it had a great effect upon him, like cocaine. He was joined by two of his friends and they too wanted cigars. I got two free glasses of tea in return. A pretty girl of about 12 came on her bicycle to the edge of the tea garden and, articulating her words with care, said: "I am pleased to meet you" like Liza Doolittle to which I replied "I am pleased to meet you too." She told me she was a Kurd and I told her I was English.

When writing up my diary after a day of travel I often begin by thinking nothing had happened worth recording but in fact it is the little things, the brief chance encounters that make it so worthwhile. Once on a three hour train journey I found myself enmeshed by a family that included three very young, noisy and energetic children whose harassed father fought a failing battle to keep them in some form of order. He never said a word to me throughout the journey though I had become increasingly irritated by their exuberant antics. When we reached our destination and emerged from the train, the father just smiled at me – an expression that said it all: "What can you expect with three small children?"

Turks who got into conversation with me constantly expressed surprise that I was travelling alone. Why alone? What was I up to? Where had I been and where was I going. So out came the map. A traveller has to adapt to circumstances and sometimes the best available cold drink was a Pepsi to which I almost became addicted. The Turks like cats or at least tolerate them and in many eating-places, big or small, three or four prowling cats were part of the establishment. Once a tiny voracious kitten clawed its way up my trousers and settled on my lap indicating its need for food so I gave it a piece of pancake and sent it on its way.

It is always interesting how each day develops. I often started by assuming the day would be routine until some wayside incident would alter this expectation – an argument in a crowded dolmus, the discovery that the town I had arrived at for my overnight stay had no hotel or inn so prolonging my search for a bed, the old man who, after the event, told me that the inn keeper had overcharged me for my room – "you are a stranger, you see", or the boy who told me he had a cold pepsi and then brought a warm one and disappeared before I could complain. Trying to sleep in a small room that overlooked the town square and being kept awake by the music and loud conversations immediately below my window. And then, the sudden quiet that descended upon the little town at midnight.

Turkey 2001

Sinop on the Black Sea coast

The mountains come down to the sea to make the coast formidable. I am not naturally gregarious but sometimes I try. Travelling in a dolmus encourages contact because if the driver knows his business he squeezes in as many passengers as the vehicle can carry and they have to accept one another as close neighbours for the duration of their journey.

In Sinop, I visited the information office where a friendly official told me that a Sinop tour was about to leave – would I like to come? I said yes. The small bus could seat 16 and was full. The information officer, it transpired, was also the bus driver and tour leader. Apart from myself there was a very handsome young man and his still more beautiful girl friend, a lively German lady of 35 to 40 who spoke good "accented" English accompanied by her twelve year old daughter while the balance of the tourists were a group of girls, all pretty, aged 18 to 20.

We drove to Ereflek, about 25 kilometres from Sinop (so much for my idea of an historical tour) where we stopped for tea. The German lady who had paired herself with me said she had lived at Hopa on the Georgian border. Then we drove for another 25 kilometres on dirt roads, which took us over a large barrage that would eventually dam the river and came to the waterfalls that were our destination.

Whenever you travel with a party – something I rarely do – there are always hiccups as people are sorted out, the slowest have to be catered for or the youngest. Our guide asked me whether I should take my walking stick as there was quite a bit of scrambling up rocks to do. I have always taken a walking stick on my walking trips – I have quite a collection of them – but most people associate walking sticks with old age!

The starting point of our walk was a sheer waterfall of maybe 100 feet into a deep pool. After scrambling up beside the waterfall we walked about one and a half miles up a marvellous little gorge with one waterfall after another to negotiate, all covered over by the foliage of high trees on either bank to provide shade from the fierce sun. Everyone became more and more friendly as they helped each other over the more difficult places. It was the wet that made for difficulty as all the rocks were splashed with water from the falls.

The handsome young man got to the head of each climb first and then helped everybody else. They all wanted to help me – the old man! I did not need help but they didn't believe it. Our guide insisted upon periodic stops for the halt and lame to get their breath The German lady insisted that she had the wrong shoes for such a scramble but she was robust and managed in spite of her shoes. Her daughter was always in the lead, vying with the handsome young man to be first.

Eventually we reached the source of the stream. We walked back along a different, easy path to a picnic area. Virtually everyone (except me) had brought food, which they cooked in special outdoor kitchens. There was a refrigerator full of cold drinks including beer, which only the tour leader and I took, the others were happy with cokes or orange juice. We sat round the long fixed table waiting for the food and the teenagers who did not know one another became great friends. The food consisted of huge rolls stuffed with meat and peppers. I took some photos. Our tour leader gave a little speech in which he said we had all been spurred on by the example of the German lay with the wrong shoes who nonetheless had persevered and me. He did not attribute my spurring them on to any special quality – my walking shoes were fine – but it was clearly understood – old age! The trip had been a fun occasion but a rarity for me because it was the sort of thing I normally avoid like the plague.

Turkey 2001

Amasya

Amasya, the capital of the province of that name in central Turkey, bestrides the Yesil Irmak (Green River) as it runs through its great gorge. For more than 200 years to 183BC it was the capital of Pontus, ruled over by the Pontic kings, Mithridates by name. In 65BC the Roman general Pompey made Amasya a free city and the administrative centre of an extensive region. It was the birthplace of Strabo and many centuries later became a favourite resort of the Ottoman Turks. It is a beautiful little city that straddles either side of the river and was long famous for its waterwheels. The ruins of a great fortress on a hilltop on one side of the city testify to its strategic importance throughout its history. Old buildings are concentrated on the south side of the river and many of these overhang the swift flowing waters of the river.

This was my third visit to Amasya. I had reached Samsun on my journey along the Black Sea coast and had determined to make a detour to Amasya, which I did by bus. The stop was on the outskirts of Amasya and I stepped from the air conditioned bus into a blast of hot air, the middle of a heatwave. First I sought a hotel: two were closed for refurbishment as Amasya was gearing itself to become a tourist destination but eventually I found what I was told was the best hotel. When I booked my room I inquired about the water wheels and was told that I would see – an odd evasion – for only one was working, the largest and grandest that had creaked all through the night on my first visit had been taken down for repairs but not replaced.

Late in the afternoon I made my way up the steep hillside to visit the Pontic tombs that had been cut into the rock face more than 2400 years ago. Only after I had visited each tomb in turn did I return to the tea garden, shaded by high trees, in the little central square. Some of the magic of my first visit had gone but the tombs and the houses overhanging the river and the swift flowing waters still made Amasya a place of wonder.

The next morning I was out early to take photos and had the little back streets, clean and silent, to myself. I visited the old mosque of the Twisted Minaret that dated from the 13th century and the old inn that was dated 1758. A grander mosque with two minarets, founded in 1485, in the reign of Sultan I Beyazit stood silent in the dawn. But the ancient rock tombs of the Pontic Kings alone conveyed a sense of the grandeur of time. Too often in history, however, it is the evil leaders and warriors who leave behind a legacy that attracts historians.

The last of the Pontic Kings, Mithridates VI Eupator, claimed descent from the first Mithridates and Darius. He was a legendary figure whose death was greeted by the Romans as though they had won a great victory. He had succeeded to the Pontic throne at the age of II (in 120 BC) but his guardians wanted to assassinate him so he became a wanderer, a fugitive in his own kingdom, where he learnt disguise, deceit and hardship at an early age, changing his sleeping place every night for fear of those who would kill him. He grew to heroic stature and was renowned for his physical accomplishments, whether as sportsman, fighter, gourmet or womaniser. He was ruthless and despotic so that even those closest to him lived in fear. He studied poisons to inure himself from their effects and to know which one to use for those he would eliminate. He was a man of boundless energy and it was this rather than statesmanship which enabled him to expand his kingdom. Sometimes he would wander incognito through the land, all of whose many languages he is said to have mastered. He was to give more trouble to the Romans, as they expanded eastwards than any other opponent until the Parthian wars.

Turkey 2001

Erzurum

More than 6,000 feet above sea level in the high country of Eastern Turkey stands the ancient city of Erzurum. In my travels I often detoured to visit places that I had read about –

attracted by the name or for some other reason – and in the case of Erzurum my interest had been fostered by reading John Buchan's most popular novel, Greenmantle, when I was twelve. Erzurum provided the setting for the climax of the story. The city is surrounded by mountains that form a natural cup and though its foundation goes back much further, it came to prominence in the fifth century as a Byzantine fortress. In subsequent centuries it was fought over and changed hands between the Byzantines, Arabs and Armenians before it fell to the Seljuq Turks in 1071. In 1515 it became part of the expanding Ottoman Empire. It was the battleground between the Turks and the Russians (1916-1918) in the Great War. The first Turkish Nationalist Congress, presided over by Mustafa Kemal (later Ataturk), was held in Erzurum and set in motion the events that saw the abolition of the Sultanate and creation of the Turkish Republic. The city pays suitable homage to Ataturk with a modern monument to Turkey's greatest hero. The centre of the city is a museum of ancient buildings. There is the 12th century Great Mosque, Seljuq theological colleges dating from the thirteenth century, a clutch of royal tombs. The grandest monument of all, commanding the centre of the city, is the Medrese or school of twin minarets. These rise on either side of the front façade. They are not capped but identical in their forbidding grandeur. From the top of an ancient bell tower one can pick out these monuments and see the spread of the city and the encircling mountains to the east and north. I spent a day examining past splendours but kept coming back to the school of twin minarets. I always enjoy wandering in an historic city but it is hungry work and in the early evening I set out to find a suitable eating place and discovered a jewel. The restaurant was near the city centre and its furnishings and mirrors were entirely art deco and I had a meal and wine to match my day.

Turkey 2001

EUROPE

Walking through Estonia

When I go on a long walk I always take with me a special book, the sort of book that I have long meant to read but for which I have never put aside the required time. On this occasion I had the Iliad translated into blank verse by the 14th Earl of Derby who for his other occupations was three times Prime Minister of England.

"Of Peleus' son, Achilles, sing, O Muse,
The vengeance, deep and deadly; whence to Greece
Unnumber'd ills arose; which many a soul
Of mighty warriors to the viewless shades
Untimely sent; they on the battle plain
Unburied lay, a prey to rav'ning dogs,
And carrion birds; but so had Jove decreed,
From that sad day when first in wordy war,
The mighty Agamemnon, King of men,
Confronted stood by Peleus' godlike son."

When booking in to fly from London to Tallin my purpose was queried by the desk clerk because I had no return ticket. She telephoned a superior official and explained that I wanted to walk! This was allowed.

It was July and the temperature was in the eighties. My first stop after Tallin was in a guesthouse built beside a large old mansion. There appeared to be no one about and I went to sit on a seat facing a pond or small lake that was surrounded by encroaching vegetation, which attracted a range of bird life. I read the Iliad aloud to myself until I found I had an audience. They were Finns – three of them – and they wanted me to provide rooms for the night. But, luckily, the landlady appeared and led them away.

I wandered round the grounds, overgrown and secretive, and came upon a white stone figure of the Virgin Mary. She was mounted on a flat stone base upon which was carved the hammer and sickle of the USSR and the dates 1941-1945 and the words 'To the Soviet War Dead'. Later that evening I discovered that the guesthouse had been built in 1937, the mansion had belonged to a German family and later (after the war) had served as an agricultural college. I asked the landlady about the Virgin Mary and whether the mansion and guesthouse had been headquarters for Soviet troops but she denied that there had ever been any Russians there. I tried again, repeating the words at the base of the Virgin Mary but she brushed this aside:

"There have never been any Russians here."

I did find in Estonia and Latvia as well as Lithuania deeply ingrained hatred of both the Germans and Russians who had changed places with each other as the occupying powers of the three little states during the war.

Estonia July 2004

Indifference and cheating

From Liepaja I meant to take the coast road to Nica, an easy 20 kilometres, but first I had a breakfast of lamphreys sitting at a table by the roadside. A German couple occupied another nearby table. I had never come across lamphreys before though I knew from my early history lessons that King John was reputed to have died from eating a surfeit of lamphreys.

Across the road was a busy stop at which a bus was taking on passengers. A well-dressed woman came running to catch the bus but as she reached the back end of it she tripped and fell flat on her face on the rain-soaked pavement. Her shopping bag spilled apples and oranges onto the road and several children who had been standing talking together now ran towards the fallen woman, as I thought to help her, but instead they snatched up the apples and oranges and ran away. A group of men who had been talking together looked on with impassive faces but made no move to help her. The woman raised herself slowly, clearly in pain, her dress all dirty from the wet pavement. She made an attempt to brush herself down and retrieved one apple and one orange that had rolled too close to her for the children to snatch. She looked round at the people who had witnessed her fall but their faces were all blank. In tears she moved painfully away. She was a Jewess. This wretched little scene reminded me of Charlie Chaplin's film The Great Dictator in which a crowd take potatoes from a stall and pelt them at a young woman.

The Nica Motel, a mile and a half from the centre of the little town, was sited among magnificent tall trees. A stream, frequented by Chinese geese, ran through its grounds and permanent tables and bench seats were a summer attraction for diners and drinkers. I enjoyed a slow relaxed lunch of calamaris and red Hungarian wine. When I asked the pretty young lady who had served me for the bill I found that she had charged me for extra wine as well as a sherry, which I had not ordered. The discrepancy between what I had ordered and what I was being charged for was too great to be ignored. As I studied the bill I could see that the waitress was becoming agitated and when I turned directly towards her she asked on a rising note that gave her away

"Is anything wrong?" She came over to my table and I pointed out the difference between what I had ordered and what she had charged me.

"Of course, it is wrong" she said, as though there had been some external intervention, and took the bill behind the counter to prepare a new one for me, as I thought. In fact she simply picked up another bill, the correct one, and brought it to me without pause. Had I not noticed or challenged the bill she would have pocketed the difference between the false bill and the actual cost of my meal. I paid her the correct amount and added a derisory tip and sullenly, caught out, she said "my pleasure." I thought that both she and the other waitress who had been a knowing spectator to the contemplated fraud should take a course in effective cheating before they tried it out on the public. **Latvia July 2004**

Politics on the Danube

I had obtained permission to travel on the barges, though not without considerable difficulty. The DGGS (the First Danube Steamship Company) had been sailing the river since 1829. I was to begin my barge journey from Regensburg on the Rosenburg. The director of the company took me to the docks and at the quayside we looked down at least six metres to the bridge of the barge from which Captain Schwebel peered before he came up to greet us. He was about 60, a short thickset grey-haired man, slow of speech, relaxed and friendly. Our cargo consisted of coal dust and the loading was both dirty and noisy. The barge was 90 metres long and carried a normal load of 1,100 to 1,200 tonnes. When the loading was completed we went down to the small mess for a late midday meal and Captain Schwebel, who prided himself on his cooking, broke four eggs into the frying pan and asked if that was sufficient or would I like six! He served himself a more modest portion and opened a bottle of red Austrian wine, but though he plied me generously with this he drank sparingly himself because he was on duty. The captain was of Hungarian origin though he had taken German citizenship three decades earlier. He had spent 28 years of his life on the Danube and spoke of the river with deep affection.

We nosed our way out of the docks into the Danube. Kilometre signs along the river bank gave the distance from the Black Sea which at that point was 2,373 kilometres (1,475 miles) distant. We registered a downstream speed of 15 kilometres an hour. Barges coming upstream could only manage four to five kilometres an hour. At tricky bends in the river the Captain would swing the wheel and there was a time lag between his actions on the bridge, for example a turn to port, and the response of the barge's prow 90 metres ahead of us. A change of direction of the prow did not appear to synchronise with the turning of the wheel. The response came a measurable time after the Captain had completed his manoeuvres on the bridge. Thus he would turn the wheel furiously to starboard but by the time the prow of the barge had also begun to swing to starboard he would be busily turning the wheel to port again. I never managed to relate the turn of the wheel (the rudder) to what the prow was doing.

When the mate relieved the Captain at the wheel he would enter – sometimes – into a conversation with me though he was capable of maintaining long silences. He talked to me about Austria or made fun of German beer-drinking habits. We passed through a number of locks to drop about nine metres each time. Although we appeared to have the river to ourselves for most of the time this was deceptive as we found whenever we stopped at a lock; then, quickly enough, we would find two or more barges had come up behind us to wait for their turn to pass through the lock.

For some of the time I sat at the prow of the barge, my presence there being a cause of astonishment to the crews of oncoming barges. By late evening the river was glassy smooth. The crew gathered in the mess to relax over their supper and have a drink before turning in. Captain Schwebel turned out to be a great talker when the mood took him. We would be off again at four-thirty in the morning. Politics and cooking were the Captain's great interests. He would look at me from under his drooping lids to size up my reaction after he had made one of his pronouncements.

"Everything", he said "depends upon the two superpowers: they have both managed to unite polyglot mixtures of people." He made it sound as though this had been achieved by sleight of hands and was not quite decent. He hankered for a union.

"A united Europe?" I asked.

"No, no!" That was not what he meant. He dismissed France, was contemptuous of Italy and thought the Scandinavians were too remote. America was to be no part of his union. What he meant was Germany, Austria, Hungary and Britain.

"That combination would be unbeatable", he said.

I asked why, if such a union were possible, we should not go for a united Europe. That he brushed aside:

"It might come one day," he said with airy disbelief, "but not for 100 years. We all distrust each other too much." Then he returned to his idea of Germany (he meant a united Germany), Austria, Hungary and Britain in a special union of their own. He was bitterly anti-Communist.

"Hitler was right about the Communists", he said.

When we got into our serious political discussion the youngest member of the crew got bored and went to bed. The first mate was only partly interested but the Yugoslav, Petrovic, came to life. Captain Schwebel, meanwhile, had opened a bottle of white wine to share with me.

The sudden roar of the engine coming to life woke me in the early hours of the morning. I went up onto the bridge in grey half-light as we nosed our way back into the channel to head downstream again. I sat silent on the bridge with the Captain. It was unbelievably peaceful. We disturbed many herons as we chugged along in the first light of day. They kept pace with us for a while then, without visible effort, flapped lazily ahead and across our prow to settle on the opposite bank of the river or to soar upwards for a longer flight to distant trees.

Summer 1986 The Danube

Ouzo

It was my second day in Crete when I began my serious walking. Much of Crete's northern coastline has been spoilt by the development of tourist attractions most of which appear to be geared to package holiday groups although in solitude I had inspected the ground plan of what was claimed to be the second largest Minoan remains in the island.

Now I was toiling uphill through a spectacular rocky gorge with great birds of prey – vultures and buzzards – displaying their white and brown wingspans as they circled overhead. Halfway through the gorge by a monastery built into the rocks I stopped at a small bar for refreshment.

I began walking again, slowly for the temperature was in the eighties. I continued to rise until I saw that the road entered a tunnel through the mountain. There was a sign that forbade pedestrians to use the tunnel and while I paused to consider what I should do a car drew up beside me and I was offered a lift. They were a friendly middle-aged couple and once we were through the tunnel they insisted they would take me to Neapolis, the next town of any importance, which was their destination. I think they assumed I was hitch hiking through Crete and it took some effort to convince them that I had come to walk.

My driver, as I thought of him, found a parking place in the centre of the town by an attractive square where the tables of a restaurant occupied half the space. They introduced themselves as Nick and Nana and insisted upon giving me lunch before I continued my walk. Nick told me that he had been asked to run for mayor in the coming municipal elections and Nana nodded her emphatic agreement with this. It was an enjoyable lunch, assisted by two bottles of wine as we discussed the European Union, tourism, the Minoan culture and the Germans. I took a photograph of my friends and promised to send them prints when I got back to England (which I did).

As we prepared to leave – Nick said he would drive me through the town to the highway where I must start walking again, he asked if I had anything to drink on my way. I took a half empty bottle of water from my rucksack and Nick promptly took it and gave it to our waiter with instructions I did not follow. He came back with a full bottle, which I put in my rucksack. Then we drove to the outskirts of the town and the highway, parting on the most friendly terms though Nick could still not understand why I should want to walk in eighty degrees of heat.

I reckoned I had 13 kilometres to cover to my intended destination. After about three kilometres – it was the first day of walking in such heat since leaving England – I stopped under the shade of a small wayside tree and took out my full bottle of water. I needed a drink to counteract with my lunchtime wine. I took the stopper off, put the bottle to my mouth, tilted it and took a long draught that burnt my mouth and throat and caused me to writhe in misery before I was able to walk again. Nick, in his kindness, had told the waiter to fill the bottle with ouzo.

Crete 2006

Walking in Crete

When on a walking excursion I never book places to stay in advance – I just find somewhere in the village or town I reach at the end of the day. Tourism has divided the island between strip development along the beach coasts and wild hill country inland, including Crete's famous gorges. Apart from the 3,500 year old Minoan palace of Knossos there are Greek, Roman, Venetian and Turkish remains, many worth a visit. There are little villages tucked away in the hills, which attain heights of 2,000 feet or more. And there are fierce offshore winds. I came to a headland 500 feet above sea level and was blown across the road. On this headland between the road and the drop to the sea was a tiny cantina that looked as though it too would be blown away though on closer inspection I saw it was sturdily built with strong foundations. Its owner was just opening it. He was a man of about 40 with a whipcord muscled body. I greeted him and had an orange juice. He had two black dogs that barked at me but nothing more threatening, and a tiny puppy.

"No customers?" I asked.

"I like to open for an hour or so to show that I am here."

"You cannot make a living out of this" and I gestured at his tiny hut. He told me his routine. He would swim for four hours one day spear fishing and on alternate days he would take his dogs – he had 11 all together he said – and hunt hares in the hills. He sold his fish and hares to the restaurants. Despite the physical effort of either swimming or hunting, he said he smoked 20 cigarettes a day. He asked my age – 74 I told him – and he said he had just buried his father who was

79. There was a good place to eat about 10 kilometres away he told me so we parted – it was to be a fishing afternoon for him.

Signs advertising Amstel beer were everywhere in Crete. I am not really a beer drinker but after every stretch of walking, the temperature never fell below 80, I would consume Amstels like water. At one village where I had found a room for the night there was some kind of fete in progress. I settled myself at the back of the crowd when a strange woman approached me to ask whether I was German.

"No, English" I replied and she congratulated me on my walking – she was German – and said she had passed me in her car on four separate occasions. She assumed, like German walkers, that I was proceeding according to a plan and was surprised when I told her that I lacked any routine. We had an Amstel.

In fact, I do have a plan: walking between 25 and 30 kilometres a day, taking a bus when necessary, becoming an Amstel addict at the end of each stretch, and on arrival at my destination searching first for a room and then for the best eating place. My serious book for Crete was Chaucer's *Canterbury Tales* and towards the end of my visit I came to the *Pardoner's Tale*: it is the first tale in which sex does not feature at all, only greed and treachery. Almost every meal I had included a tomato salad made with the giant tomatoes that are grown in the huge ugly plastic hothouses that mar the south coast.

I finished at the western end of Crete and spent my last day walking to the acropolis of Polyrrinia whose remains on the top of a peaked mountain were visible from miles away. The walk there was an easy 15 kilometres. Half way up to the remains of the acropolis a village offered refreshments; the subsequent path to the top was guarded by a ferocious dog on a chain. The Greek and Roman remains were hardly spectacular though most intriguing were the tanks of limpidly clear water. I returned along the gorge that paralleled the road.

Crete, June 2006

Tirana to Split

Arrived in Tirana by a late evening flight – discussions with five taxi drivers before I found one who knew where to go – walked the dusty city which is not inspiring: they are obsessed with Mother Teresa. My intention was to move north along the Adriatic coast until I reached Trieste – Kruje, high in the hills, dominated by great tower of old castle (not much else remains) – bought a walking stick to add to my collection – hotel building activity as Kruje intends to be a tourist attraction – a small museum mainly concerned with warfare – an abundance of butterflies, bees and sparrows – I became increasingly aware of sparrows, their frequency making up for their disappearance in Britain. I began walking through a great conifer forest – a boy high up in one of the trees shouted a greeting to me – out of the forest and into the flat – a little shop where I had an orange drink – although there was an elderly man behind the counter all the business was done by a girl of fifteen who informed me in good English, "He is my Dad."

My intention of walking up the Dalmatian coast was thwarted by the almost continuous road building activity as the Balkans restored or improved their capacity to earn money from tourism that had been interrupted by the wars of the 1990s. What I had thought from my maps would be walkable B roads were instead being turned into A roads to shift the rapid increase in traffic using them. There were no sidewalks and walking was increasingly hazardous and not enjoyable.

Sparrows! My room in one hotel had a balcony that was an attraction for the endlessly circling house martins; in two ceiling corners they had made nests and their droppings formed little mountains at either end of my balcony.

The town of Schkoder was more impressive than Tirana. Its main square had two mosques and an Orthodox Cathedral. In a park that was full of people relaxing I watched a group of men playing dominos and invariably at the end of a round they almost came to blows. I could not decide what made dominos such a fierce game. Sparrows in and out among the pigeons to snatch the crumbs that were clearly provided on a daily basis. Freed of Titoism, communism and civil war the Balkans, for a change, appeared ready to try out capitalism. Through Montenegro and into Croatia and so to the "Jewel" of the Adriatic – Dubrovnik.

Dubrovnik is the number one attraction on the coast and is self-consciously aware of this. I paid 10 euros to walk on its medieval walls and there are a lot of them. At a resting place where drinks were for sale I sat at a table and watched the tourists. A group of well-ordered Japanese came by, matched always in pairs and each pair bowed to me as they passed my table. When they had gone a middle-aged pair (English) asked the barman to take a picture of them. Then the woman bared her false teeth at me in a gesture of camaraderie:

"We are all having such a time", she said.

I went down to the port to look at the launches taking people on sea trips but after watching people crammed three in a row, packed body to body, I gave up. The pressure of sardined people would more than counteract the pleasure of a sea breeze. Dubrovnik lives off its beauty but what does it do when there are no tourists? Visitors come for sun and food and 'adventure' while too often the waiters are blasé and arrogant: "we will pander to your self-esteem – at a price." Everything in our capitalist world is about money and greed – and this is reflected in the tourist industry. What happens when the tourist industry collapses?

I found Split more exciting than Dubrovnik and more to my taste. It is a busy city in which tourism is an incidental activity, not the lifeblood of the whole.

Dioclitian's fortress-palace is in the centre of a bustling town with shops and markets enclosing it. The palace is massive, squatting on the waterfront, a monument to power and impregnable behind its great walls. Dioclitian's decision to divide the empire (which had become increasingly unwieldy for its rulers) ushered in a new age. Wealth and power had been steadily shifting to the east. He split the empire, making Rome the capital of the Western Empire, which was declining in influence, while Byzantium (soon to be renamed Constantinople to honour his successor Constantine the Great) became the capital of the Eastern Empire.

Diocletian, who ruled from 284 to 305, resigned the purple in the 21st year of his reign, and retired to live in the fortress he had built at Split. He had split the empire so that there were two Augusti or senior Emperors and two Caesars or junior emperors under them. The Augustus of the Eastern Empire (Dioclitian) retained overall power. He was the only Roman Emperor to retire from his position voluntarily. The second Augustus Maximian and the two Caesars were forced to retire when Dioclitian did so but Maximian was desperate to regain power – meanwhile the Empire was wracked by civil war as various contenders fought to replace the outgoing emperors.

According to Edward Gibbon in his The Decline and Fall of the Roman Empire Diocletian in retirement "developed a taste for the most innocent as well as natural pleasures, and his leisure hours were sufficiently employed in building, planting, and gardening. His answer to Maximian is deservedly celebrated. He was solicited by that restless old man to reassume the reins of government and the imperial purple. (This would allow Maximian to do the same). He rejected the temptation with a smile of pity, calmly observing that, if he could show Maximian the cabbages which he had planted with his own hand at Salona, he should no longer be urged to relinquish the enjoyment of happiness for the pursuit of power." The greatness of the work in creating his palace suggests that he had contemplated resigning the purple for some years before he actually did so.

Today this massive Roman monument is not isolated from public life but is surrounded and enmeshed in the activities of the city with shops and markets all round it. Quadrangular in shape it covers 10 acres of ground and is flanked by 16 towers. Two sides are 600 feet in length, the other two are 700 feet. It is an awe-inspiring building that has outlasted the destruction of so many monuments. The Golden Gate opens onto the market place.

Adriatic Coast, June 2010

Vodka

I took the Orient Express from Istanbul and though it lacked the grandeur of past days it still conveyed a sense of adventure. It was a great train that had seen better times before the Second World War and subsequent recuperative drabness had reduced it to the level of a European curiosity. In Istanbul the railway runs along the shoreline of the Bosporus parallel to but outside the Emperor Theodosius' giant walls. Mine was a nostalgia trip on a railway that had become outdated. We rumbled along gently from European Turkey into Bulgaria. The attendant took our passports for the border crossing. The woodwork of the carriages had the air of solidity of a past age even if the polish had gone. I made my way to the dining car and was given a seat on the aisle across from a table for four occupied by boisterous Russians. They greeted me and then settled down to eating, having come to the dining car two courses ahead of me. The Russians were army officers and whatever their business they were set to enjoy themselves. The waiter cleared their table and then brought four small glasses and a bottle of Vodka. The serious part of their meal now began with a round of toasts, first to each other and then they included me – the waiter had already provided me with a fresh glass. Then we got down to it. We toasted Russia but not the Soviet Union then England. Then we toasted our families, our parents, any brothers or sisters we could lay claim to, absent friends, and then the toasts became more random. It was the toasting that mattered. Our glasses were small, of thick glass designed for the occasion. I signalled the waiter and ordered another bottle of vodka but in unison my four Russian friends insisted that they should supply the drink – "he our guest" they told the waiter. I have a fairly strong head but at last knew I had to leave – I settled my bill and shook hands all round before weaving my way out of the dining car and to my cabin, leaving the Russians settling down to an all night session. I found my cabin, was violently sick and went to bed. During the night I woke to find the attendant cleaning the floor. Deeply ashamed of my vodka sickness I gave him a 10 deutschmark note at which he looked happier. I went back to sleep. About ten the following morning we stopped in a large station, where the train would go out the way it came in – I think it was Bucharest – and I descended to take a slow walk up and down the long platform to clear my head. As my perambulation brought me for the second time alongside the dining car the waiters, four of them, came out and stood in a line to clap me in gentle unison as I passed. Their amiable accolade completed my recovery.

Rumania 1986

The start to a long walk

When I booked in to Estonian Airlines in London, the girl asked me for my return ticket. I said I was walking. Not trained to deal with this eventuality she went away to telephone higher authority, which allowed that I could walk without hindrance. In the plane I sat beside a young businessman who was intrigued when I told him I intended to walk. He worked in Tallinn. He told me the people were friendly and pleasant and that they were going through an anti-colonial, anti-Russian mood now that the impositions of communism had been lifted. In Tallinn I took a taxi to my hotel – the only stopping place that I had booked in advance and after a nightcap in a glitzy bar I retired for the night. It was just midnight. I spent my first day in the country exploring Tallinn. It was a cold, wet day and I lost my way more than once when my wanderings took me away from the Old City. By midmorning the tourists were out in force seeking refreshments or SOUVENIIR. By the end of the day I had quartered the city and wanted to be moving.

My first problem was to find my way out of Tallinn whose suburban stretches were all alike. I walked until 5.30pm, only stopping for coffee or directions while my leg joints began to ache at the unaccustomed strains that a first long walk had put upon them. I covered 40 kilometres that first day. I had come to a village off the main road that looked more inviting than the highway. In an inn, which had been recommended to me, I obtained a bowl of soup but they were not prepared for people to stay. The nearest village with an inn or boarding house was 20 kilometres away. I asked about taxis but there were none. I ordered a beer and contemplated. The girl was sympathetic but had nothing to suggest. Then a young man swaggered in – we were in an otherwise empty dining room – who was cultivating what he thought was a western European or American manner – his hair was en brosse. He wore jeans and a T-shirt and swung a bunch of keys. He was the girl's boyfriend and at her indication they left the room in a huddle and had a talk in the adjacent huge banqueting room. She returned to tell me he would take me in his car to Depla where they assured me there was accommodation. I asked how much and she disappeared again into the banqueting hall to return a couple of minutes later to say the price they had decided: was 200 Estonian Kroons. Slowly I followed the young man down the stairs – the empty restaurant was on the first floor – and I was so stiff that I could hardly maintain my balance. The young man had an old, well-used Mercedes and would take me to the hotel in Depla.

It was a swift, easy journey; my driver only had a scrap of English so I enjoyed the journey in silence. But when we drove up to the front of what appeared to be an old established hotel I knew we were in trouble since the veranda, which fronted the hotel was occupied by three geriatrics in wheel chairs.

"Do not worry", said my driver, almost the first sentence he had uttered and then he got out of the car and went in search of advice. The hotel had been turned into a Rest Home for the aged. He returned after a few minutes, got into the car and indicated there was a boarding house close by. He took me there and told me to stay in the car while he checked that there was a room. There was! I paid him the K200 as agreed and he gave me a cheery goodbye and drove away. It was a pleasant boarding house and the woman in charge spoke English. I had a shower and changed and then went into the lounge where I had a brandy and wrote up my travel notes. Critics of my walking habits would say that my problems arose entirely from my habit of not booking a room in advance. They may well be right but I preferred to allow my day to develop in its own way.

Estonia summer 2004

ASIA/EUROPE

Breakfast in Amman

We had crossed the border from Iraq into Jordan: there was very little sign of a border and formalities had been minimal. I was catching up on time after a long delay in Tehran and wanted to reach London by mid-December, as did my co-driver Alan. We had filled up with petrol and were looking for the road, supposedly a straight run to Amman, but all we could see was sand. There was a big, jolly Jordanian ahead of us, clearly amused by our bafflement.

"Just follow me", he said, pointing at tyre marks leading away from the border crossing. The sun had already gone down and we decided to drive all night. Following Mohamed – we discovered his name later – was no easy matter for he had a large saloon car and drove it at 60 miles or more all the time. We drove a long wheel-base Landrover whose maximum speed was 60. Mohamed would drive into the night desert and I would follow his lights. These, however, would keep disappearing although we were driving across flat desert all the time. Sometimes Mohamed would wait and then, as our lights approached him he would start up and race off again; sometimes we would find vision obscured by night sand-mists and I was constantly worried that Mohamed would finally disappear and we would get lost in the desert.

That night drive in pursuit of Mohamed was one of the most difficult I could remember. Twice we caught up with a stationary Mohamed who suggested a rest but he was too restless and after a few minutes, or so it seemed, he would start off and the pursuit would begin again.

It was after three in the morning that I became conscious of an ominous clicking noise sounding above the engine. We came to a stationary Mohamed who told us there was a little shed about five miles ahead where we could get a drink of tea and then he was in his car and away again. The five miles seemed endless and the clicking got louder until we came up with Mohamed who was standing by his car in front of a dilapidated small holder shed whose owner had just been roused and was making tea. I stayed in the driving seat and asked Mohamed if he would listen to our clicks.

"Drive forward slowly" he said and I did – two clicks- and he said "stop" and bent down to examine the front wheel. Four of the five bolts that attached the wheel to the hub had sheered off and only one bolt stood between us and disaster. Had the fifth bolt sheered off, as it would have done before much longer, we would have ended upside down and at 60 mph that would have been fatal.

I wondered how long we would be stranded in the desert waiting for mechanical assistance to come but Mohamed was quite cheerful. As though he understood my fears he said, "I'll ask the old man." They had a discussion, the old man came to examine the wheel by torchlight and then disappeared into the back of his shed. He produced tea for us and Mohamed said, "do not worry, he will fix it."

I thought of the four large bolts needed to replace those that had sheered off but divining my thought Mohamed said: "He has everything, you wait and see."

After two hours and ten cigarettes, the wheel with five new bolts was ready for service. I settled with the old man and we mounted our vehicles and set off for Amman as the sun rose behind us and the desert became bathed in light. We went to Mohamed's house and his wife within minutes had produced breakfast: hot fresh bread straight from the oven, a bowl of olive oil and another of crushed nuts. We took a piece of bread, dipped it in the olive oil and then in the nuts. It was a splendid breakfast to cap a nerve-wracking night.

November 1964 Jordan

Georgia: seeking accommodation

Georgia in 2001 was not exactly geared to accommodate visitors. Batum was reasonable, Poti boasted a number of grandiose public buildings of the Soviet era and a magnificent opera house standing alone and unused but hotel accommodation was a different matter and I was happy after a miserable night to secure a seat in a dolmus going to Kataisi. Reached Kataisi by 10.20am. Walked down a long wide avenue of dilapidated blocks, crumbling road, indifferent shops and many empty buildings. I could not find a centre or even a little restaurant for breakfast. Eventually came to a lokanta and took a seat at a table facing the street. Almost at once a waiter brought me a jug of beer. Tea, I said, but no, so beer it had to be. When I went to pay the woman who had now taken up her place behind the bar shook her head and pointed to a table where four men sat and I realised they had presented me with the beer because I was a stranger. I acknowledged their courtesy but no one had heard of the town's only hotel, which I had been assured existed.

The general dilapidation made one wonder what communism had ever done for Georgia. Eventually an English-speaking taxi driver told me of the old hotel Tskaltubo that was 15 kilometres outside the city. In Soviet times it had been the only place where foreigners were allowed to stay. The drive to Tskaltubo was through lush green countryside and the hotel was a demonstration of Stalinist architecture. A woman in black greeted me. She took me to the office where I produced my passport and signed myself in. She was both friendly and polite and spoke reasonable English but there was an unmistakable air about her as she summed me up, a whiff of an earlier Stalinist era. She led me to my room, which was bright, high-ceilinged and spacious. "We go in to lunch at two o'clock" she told me so I had a shower and changed before writing up my diary.

Down in the hall a little man sitting there indicated that the dining room was in a different building altogether and he would come with me. He was a cripple I saw as soon as he stood. Lunch was served in an open-sided rotunda where a number of tables were already laid. My guide introduced me to the woman who presided over the restaurant.

"The English man" she said and showed me to a small table laid for one where I was served an excellent plain meal.

There was vaguely scented water to drink but no strong liquor was served so that I imagined Soviet times when overworked bureaucrats had come here to restore their health without the aid of vodka. Other guests consisted of big heavy men and bigger heavier women. They looked sullen and, whatever the reality, as though they were still Soviet citizens enjoying holidays for members of the party who were in good standing. In the afternoon they dutifully walked through the grounds and admired the other buildings of this elegantly cared for retreat. I couldn't help thinking they might have preferred Blackpool. It was a spa, I learnt, and so they came to take the waters.

I found my way to a small secluded garden where the centre was adorned with a marble plinth on which a gold head and shoulders young-appearing Stalin looked on all who passed. Though he had been denounced elsewhere, in Georgia he was still revered. Although the grounds were beautiful the grandiose period piece buildings showed distinct signs of neglect; at the very least they needed a fresh coat of paint. I met two of the large – though not largest – women from the next table who indicated that supper was at seven o'clock so I followed them to the restaurant for a meal of mashed potatoes, a form of burger and a vegetable/rice mixture followed by a pasta milk pudding (very tasty) and a large glass of tea and a jug of iced water. One of the women gave me two sweets to go with the tea. One of the men then came to sit at my table to ask where I was going. He told a story of marching behind a leader and indicated a moustache in a clear reference to Stalin. Then he laughed and went away.

Outside on the terrace I asked the two women to pose for

a photo and two others – a mother and daughter –joined us. Then an even larger lady joined us to have her photo taken. They had all come from Batum and were Azerbaijanis. The astonishing thing about Tskaltubo, which must have been a showplace in Communist times, is that though the hotel was comfortable and the food adequate the guests were all regimented as to time while half the buildings were in disrepair and not used. After another wander round the extensive grounds I returned to the main building to find my five big ladies sitting in a row on the veranda. The auburn haired mother gave me two glasses of ice cold water to drink – "raqi", I said and the men, who were sitting apart all laughed. Then the daughter appeared with a camera and took two pictures of me and her mother. I retired to my room to write. After a miserable night in Poti and an awful morning in Kataisi this would-be Eden, presided over by the ghost of Stalin – had proved wonderfully restful.

Georgia 2001

The military road to Russia and Qazbegi

In the wide open centre of Tbilisi – Republic Square – is a podium from which leaders and grandees review parades on such occasions as Mayday. Behind the podium stand nine tall arches like upended coffins, aptly described as Andropov's ears in the dying days of communism. Tbilisi, founded in the mid-fifth century has a history stretching through centuries of invasions by Persians, and Byzantines, and Arabs and Mongols and Timur and the Turks who have captured and sacked it before adding it to their empires until finally it became part of the Soviet Empire, noted as the birthplace of both Stalin and the hateful Beria, and developed as a holiday resort for tired communist aparatchniks. The ancient citadel has unique patterns worked into its brick walls and beyond it on a high ridge stands, in white stone, the huge symbolic figure of Georgia. The Russians built the Military Highway to link Georgia to their empire and the journey down this highway from Russia to Georgia is described by both Pushkin and Tolstoy in their writings, so I decided to make an excursion down the military highway. Fifteen minutes from the centre of Tbilisi the dolmus entered the military road. The passengers were all men and friendly. The valley soon narrowed to become spectacular and we rose in height as we headed for the Caucasus Mountains. At first the hills were tree covered but before long the trees gave way to open turf and rocks and ridges not unlike the Aonoch Eiger Ridge of Glencoe in Scotland. At one point we came through a pass in the mist at 6,000 feet.

At eleven o'clock we stopped at a little roadside market and watering place presided over by a stone icon engraved in a towering rock. Four Russian men, as well as the driver of the dolmus had decided to befriend me. We sat round a trestle table. What will you have to drink they asked me. Tea I said. They laughed: vino! They produced bread and huge tomatoes, which the driver, acting as host, cut up. From one of the little stores a woman brought us warmed bread filled with cheese. Over some 25 minutes while the driver, correct if wistful, refused to drink, the other four men and myself quaffed four bottles of a local but superior rose. Unfortunately for enjoyment the wine was all drunk in single shots, a whole glass full at a time as toast after toast was proposed: Georgia; Anglia; our families; God – in that order. During the first part of the drive to this market we had passed several orthodox churches and one of the men, rather cautiously, had crossed himself. From this point onwards, joined by a second of the foursome, they ostentatiously crossed themselves, forgetting the restrictions in years only just past. Later, on the road to Qazbegi, an argument developed that I could only just understand whose gist was that more progress had been made under Stalin and the communist regime than now when the former Soviets like Tajikistan were going their own way and not doing well.

The main defender of communism turned to me and said: "Fidel Castro – good", and his forefinger went up in the air.

Yes I said, agreeing with my finger;

"Stalin good", he continued, pointing his finger upwards. Yes, I said and raised my finger very slowly and they all laughed. It was a wonderful, winding road as we constantly came to hairpin bends in the mist that the driver took at maximum speed. We came to Qazbegi and I got out with my rucksack and walking stick and the four who were continuing to Russia a few miles further on stood in a row for me to photograph.

I asked directions to the ECO as it was called, a WWF centre that acted as a hotel when not full of scientists. I climbed a steep hill to the ECO and enjoyed spectacular views of the mountains while imbibing sharp fresh air. A young woman explained that I must wait for the manager to return before she could give me a room but meanwhile gave me coffee and flapjacks and rhubarb jam and butter. After a rest – the young lady let me into a room after all – I went out to explore. There was little to see except the fast running waters of the river going towards Russia, and a little dilapidated church with a huge urn beside it. High up on a mountain ridge stood a tiny church that I decided to visit. To do so I had to pass through a cluttered village on the hillside (whether an extension of Qazbegi or not I never discovered). I asked an old man, sign language, whether the path led to the church and he signalled yes and gave a zigzag sign. It took me two hours to reach the church which was on a spur of the mountain and the land fell away sharply behind it down to a sparkling stream may be 1,000 feet below. The church was ancient with patterns worked into its brick walls while the views from it in all directions were magnificent. I had reached the church at 4.30 after two hours climb. At 18 minutes to five I began the descent into the village where I purchased grapes and peaches at a tiny fruit market. The director Osmat was back. He was a slow-speaking, pleasant man and we had a conversation about the conservation work for which he was responsible. A young Norwegian couple were staying in the ECO beside me. Supper was excellent, especially the soup, but there was altogether too much food, a response to mountain climbers who always come back hungry at the end of the day.

The next morning I arranged with Epson and Lila, the Norwegian couple, to make an excursion up the Sno valley and Osmat promised to arrange a driver and land rover to take us. Down the valley and just before the village of Sno we passed some sculptures by local artists in the 19th century – huge white stones, eight or nine feet high, standing upright with faces carved into the surface of the stones. We continued up the valley to Djuta, the highest village in the region at 2,200m, inhabited by the Khevsor families. In the distance ahead of us to the east were the rugged peaks of Chankhi reaching 3,842m with 2,400 feet cliffs. We were approaching Chechnya and came to two military tents. They were manned by five young soldiers who demanded to see our passports but were friendly. We continued for another 300 yards until the road petered out. We sat on the bank of the small river to eat the pack lunches Osmat had supplied. The water of the stream was clear and the sun made the mountains stand out sharply. It would be bleak in winter! When we came to Djuta again Epson and I walked up into the village which was clustered away from the road but apart from a group of hikers with packs, resting, no villagers appeared: they had retreated from the influx of strangers although our driver told us they would all be out cutting hay but we saw no sign of this. Back at the ECO we enjoyed an excellent supper and retired early. I planned to climb a far as the Glacier on Qazbegi Mountain. There were other climbers about and I fell in with two for a time. They may have been good mountaineers – I did not find out – but both were panting with effort half the time and I left them at one of our resting places where they said they would eat their lunch. I began my return to the ECO at 3pm having reached the foot of the glacier. On my descent I again visited the little church – no one else was there – and rested enjoying the beautiful sound of silence. Further down by the path were some iron tables and at one sat three men enjoying a feast. They hailed me and insisted I should join them. I said I wanted water and then one of them, a huge young man who spoke a little English, gave me a glass of ice-cold vodka. I was not really hungry but they insisted upon plying me with their food – cut sausages, tomatoes, salami and little sardines out of tins. I do not think they had any serious climbing in mind. Then we toasted one another, the bottle emptied but they got another out of the stream so the vodka was again icy cold. After three vodkas I presented them each with a cigar and escaped and made my way down to the little hillside village and up the other side of the valley to the ECO which I reached at 6pm. I left for Tbilisi the next morning, sorry to leave Osmat and my Norwegian friends but I had a timetable to keep. The military road looked quite different when travelling it back to Tbilisi and with a road carved out of the hillside it was an easier proposition than the old pictures I had seen of the gorge when Pushkin, Tolstoy and Lementov travelled it when the only path was immediately beside the river so that the rising rocks of the gorge would have looked especially dramatic. At one picturesque point a cross had been erected. An ancient man wearing a floppy hat and a kind of smock had been tending the ground round the cross and was walking towards us where we had stopped so that I could take a photo.

Georgia 2001

Into Iran

With my travelling companion Alan, we arrived at the Afghan-Iran border in the late afternoon in time to see an enormous black cloud, like a wall a thousand feet tall, advancing on us from Iran. The temperature dropped dramatically as we secured what we could before we were enveloped in a sandstorm. When that had passed we approached the border controls which at that time were lax and friendly. On the Afghan side we were presented with a list of about1000 books that were banned in the interests of purity and we assured them we had no books of such a nature with us. On the Iranian side we were informed that the price of petrol had been doubled that very day by decree of the Shah.

The landrover was beginning to make odd noises so I drove it up a rugged hill and turned it to face downwards so that we could start it without too much trouble in the morning. It proved a wise precaution. There had been a fall of snow during the night that had covered everything with a thin white shroud. It was a dirt road with potholes as a regular feature. We came round a corner to be confronted with a huge dead boar occupying the centre of the road, covered in snow to provide it with a decent shroud. Then the engine spluttered and went dead. Neither of us had any mechanical aptitude and after peering under the bonnet for a sign we stood pondering what to do.

A crowded bus now came round the corner and stopped behind our vehicle. All the men got out to greet us and ask what was wrong. One man who spoke English told us what was best to do in that remote area – no garages for many miles he said before recommending that we drove very slowly but not to let the engine stop which was easier to say than for us to do. The crawling journey took us two days and what I mainly remember was that we consumed endless dishes of yoghurt as our primary source (affordable) of energy. We were, he informed us with a humorous glint in his eye, 600 kilometres from Tehran.

Finally, we drove into Tehran and in the centre of what I calculated was the Piccadilly Circus of Tehran the landrover gave a shudder and settled down for good. Horns blared round us and we were cursed in more than one language.

And then a beaming, friendly face appeared at my window and its owner said in English: "Do not worry, I feex" and he bobbed out of sight as though he had a ready toolbox with him.

Soon, however, his face now expressive of sorrow, he appeared at my window to say: "Sorry, no feex". Then the police arrived to tell us there was a landrover garage in Tehran and they had sent for a vehicle to tow us to it. We found accommodation and spent a pleasant week as sightseers in Iran's capital while the landrover was checked and restored to full working order – by then we had covered about 7000 miles on mainly dirt roads. We started again, first destination Iraq.

Iran October 1964

A MISCELLANY 10

Glencoe: the North Face

Training to be an officer (National Service) at Eaton Hall, Chester, we were given five days leave. I decided to hitch hike to Scotland, I had never been there before, and climb a mountain. It rained all day as I walked the road beside Loch Lomond but at Tarbet, as instructed by my friend Barry, I found an old man (Angus by name) who rowed me across the loch to have lunch with Barry and his father the laird. The Loch was choppy and the rain intermittently heavy – I thought of Walter Scott's poem "I am the Lord of Ulva's Isle and this Lord Ullin's daughter". After an excellent lunch Barry Senior invited us both to visit the attic. This was huge and presented a bare floor covered with lead soldiers of every regiment and formation of the British army through the ages. Barry Senior spent a happy hour explaining to me the intricacies of the British regimental system. I intended to spend the night at The Kingshouse which had been a base for General Wade as he built roads into the Highlands after the 45 rebellion. The ancient inn, as I discovered, appeared not to have changed since Wade's time. A ferry went to the head of the Loch. I took this and on disembarkation found a man who would give me a lift to the Kingshouse. Barry Senior had warned me that accommodation at the Kingshouse was limited but he gave me a "chit" addressed to the then manager who had formerly been on his staff. He found a camp bed for me in an outhouse. I was in uniform and pressed my trousers by arranging them under the sheets and sleeping on them.

After a mug of tea and porridge I departed to climb the Buchaille Etive Mor. I set off down the Glen Etive road and then, as instructed, cut up the rear side of the Buchaille whose spectacular north side faced the Kingshouse. It rained for most of that day although there were occasional breaks that allowed a view of the gloomy glen. I was fit (military training) and reached the summit by mid-afternoon. There was a break in the rain that allowed me to see the Glen and the Kingshouse from where I had started.

But rain threatened and I began my descent. The edge of the forbidding North Face looked practicable and I made steady progress downwards, unaware of the treachery of mountain climbing until I got stuck at the end of an inviting ledge that I had followed. I did not want to retrace my steps and thought I could manage to pass a rock outcrop that barred my way. My rucksack was an encumbrance for what I intended to do so I took it off and the strap ran though my numbed hand and the next moment I saw my rucksack bounding down the gully to come to a stop, obligingly, in a stream. An hour later, having unconsciously ignored all the rules of mountain walking or climbing I reached my rucksack. My change of clothing was all soaked and my sandwiches ruined. Eventually, by then the rain had turned to sleet, I reached the road down to Glencoe village. I enveloped myself in my army poncho and sat on a convenient rock, shivering with cold but pleased too that I had conquered the mountain – in a manner of speaking.

A young man on a motorbike came to a halt beside me and offered to give me a lift to the village. There was nowhere to stay that I could afford but I bought some frugal provisions including matches and sought a small empty shed that my motorcycle friend had told me about. There I made a fire, had some supper and curled up for the night.

Two days later back in Eaton Hall I was put on a charge for not wearing my military (blancoed) belt which had been damaged when it went down the mountain side attached to my rucksack. In subsequent years people who know Scotland have told me they found Glencoe too grim, but for me, having visited it many times since, it remains the dramatic gateway into the Scottish Highlands. **Scotland, April 1951**

"White" Bermuda 1960

An island of contrasting colours – houses painted in pastels – stepped white roofs to catch the rain – wonderful blue sky against the green sea. Bermuda became a British colony in 1612 and its white population flaunts this fact. I went there for a holiday and to visit an aunt. I found the island to be a curious mixture of English and non-English and soon discovered that I was conducting a personal anthropological study of my own. The cars were British marques, and the shops in the centre of Hamilton displayed British made goods but in parallel were American cigarettes and the extensive use of the dollar. The long-established British entrepreneurs were collectively known as "The Forty Thieves". The economy depended upon tourism and that meant the steady influx of American holidaymakers. Conversations turned on money and who had it, evading British taxes for new arrivals, and the split personality of the Island that wanted to remain British but was fascinated by the American dollar. Seeping through these economic concerns I soon became engaged in exploring the prevalent race issues that underlay the colony's life style. About 14 years prior to my visit the churches (mainly Anglican) had played their part in the race divide. In Church the whites sat on one side, the blacks on the other and the blacks remained kneeling when the whites went forward for communion. Since then – an advance – people were able to sit as they liked, mixed race or not. In the 1950s the black population had discovered and then perfected the art of boycott, a weapon that was conducive to change. The Bishop had argued that only time could bring about a change of attitude. I made friends with a talkative travel agent who prefaced his comments – entre nous – before providing me with more information. How was the colour bar assisted by the tourist industry? All US and Canadian travel agents, he told me, used code words when booking hotels in Bermuda – G for geranium, H for Hibiscus - G was for Jews, H for blacks and only certain hotels would accept bookings for Gs or Hs. If there had been a slip and a G or an H turned up at the hotel of his choice fulsome apologies were offered: there had been a double booking. Only certain hotels would accept G or H bookings. I arranged to meet with representatives of the Visitors' Service Bureau and the Hotel and Guest House Association and in each case I asked about accommodation for Jews or Blacks. My questions were answered reluctantly while I was regarded askance for my temerity in seeking such information. A special brochure for black holiday makers to Bermuda provided a list of hotels and guest houses where they could stay while the front of the brochure showed cheerful blacks being received against a background of sea and palm trees.

A word of admonition: "Bermuda, like other places where you live for instance – has its ideas too of what are good manners in dress. The correct shorts to wear outdoors are Bermuda shorts, which are cut just above the knee."

"Blacks" I was told by the manager of a big hotel, were allowed in to eat but not to stay. Underneath the many prohibitions that reinforced the racial segregation – never openly discussed – was the fear of trans-racial sexual relations. The manager confirmed how they knew a booked person to be black.

"We all have representatives at travel agencies who tell blacks that they cannot stay at certain places. I am English so I know how you feel" he told me, employing a new line in explaining the company's racial policy.

"Bermuda has economic problems and cannot afford to offend its major source of visitors who come from the American South.

As another hotelier put it: "We all know it is coming any way (Racial integration), so why push it?"

Racial snobbery was deeply embedded in the Island's history and recently, I was told, an English girl had been deported for going out with a Chinese man – "We cannot allow such behaviour.

The Bermuda Naval station has a long history. Able Bodied sailors of the Royal Navy hated being stationed in Bermuda: the Island was so snobbish and ABs were never invited anywhere and there was nothing to do so they remained on board. **Bermuda 1960**

Albuquerque

The largest city in New Mexico, pretty nearly the centre of the United States, Albuquerque had been occupied and turned into an army base by the United States in 1846. Since the 1930s 100 Federal agencies and institutions had been located there while after 1945 it had been the centre for aerospace and solar research industries including the Sandia Laboratories and base, a major air base and the Defence Atomic Support Agency and others. In other words, in 1965 – just three years after the Cuban Missile Crisis – it was a spies delight. I touched down in Albuquerque in July of that year, was met by David who had arranged for my visit in London a month earlier and driven the 100 miles north of the city to an army camp where I would be lecturing for the next three weeks. The army camp was now used for group training for work in the developing world that the United States was just beginning to take seriously. My audience consisted of 40 young Africans from newly independent countries who were considered to be leadership material. Higher authority had insisted through David that I supplied an outline of my course – that is, notes for each of the 12 lectures I was to deliver. David had assured me that these would be printed and assembled in book form for me to hand out as I saw fit.

The camp was self-sufficient: it had to be since it was located in bleak scrub desert territory. There were other small groups being trained or lectured but I had nothing to do with them. There was a middle-aged camp follower who dressed like a cowboy and insisted that everyone knew him – they call me 'Red' he said. There was an attractive girl in her teens who rode through the camp everyday and off to some destination in the shrub land. There was a muscular young marine who demonstrated to me how hard their training was by jumping up to grab the branch of a tree and do pull ups. He made such a business of this – he had large biceps – that in the end, when he was resting, I who did not possess large biceps nevertheless jumped up to grasp his branch and do twice as many pull-ups as he so that, disgruntled, he drifted.

David, and I noticed a certain diffidence about him, brought to my cabin the bound copies of my lecture notes. The outlines of my two first lectures had been omitted. These as far as I was concerned, were the most important of the whole and between them covered the activities of the major powers in Africa and how new African states had to break free of neo-colonial manipulations. I looked at David who blushed and looked furtive but finally said the CIA had insisted they were not on the record.

"Too frank?" I said.

"You can lecture as you please", he said but – and he shrugged his shoulders: "that is how it is in these days." I should not have been surprised but I was. I had a lot to learn.

There was a young French man, Paul, who was lecturing another group and one afternoon, lectures finished, military lunch consumed, we decided to hire a taxi and visit Albuquerque 100 miles to the south. We did some obligatory sight seeing, arranged with the taxi a place to pick us up for the return journey and then, on his recommendation went to the best nightclub in town. It was a dance night and some ferocious hick dancing was underway. We sat at a small table against a wall and watched the scene before us. A waiter brought us beer and through the evening would reappear just as we finished our glasses with fresh beers. Paul was as political as I and we discussed the management of the Cold War and what was likely to happen in Africa. Paul took pride in reminding me that President de Gaulle had told the Americans to remove their NATO bases from French soil. Then he became transfixed by the scene before us – men in braces dancing energetically, shouting and sweating, and could restrain himself no longer. He waved his hand in a sweeping gesture that embraced the whole scene before us and said: "And it is these people whose finger is on the nuclear trigger."

United States 1965

TRAILBLAZER TITLE LIST

Adventure Cycle-Touring Handbook
Adventure Motorcycling Handbook
Australia by Rail
Australia's Great Ocean Road
Azerbaijan
Coast to Coast (British Walking Guide)
Cornwall Coast Path (British Walking Guide)
Corsica Trekking – GR20
Cotswold Way (British Walking Guide)
The Cycling Anthology
Dolomites Trekking – AV1 & AV2
Dorset & Sth Devon Coast Path (British Walking Gde)
Exmoor & Nth Devon Coast Path (British Walking Gde)
Hadrian's Wall Path (British Walking Guide)
Himalaya by Bike – a route and planning guide
Inca Trail, Cusco & Machu Picchu
Japan by Rail
Kilimanjaro – the trekking guide (includes Mt Meru)
Morocco Overland (4WD/motorcycle/mountainbike)
Moroccan Atlas – The Trekking Guide
Nepal Trekking & The Great Himalaya Trail
New Zealand – The Great Walks
North Downs Way (British Walking Guide)
Offa's Dyke Path (British Walking Guide)
Overlanders' Handbook – worldwide driving guide
Peddars Way & Norfolk Coast Path (British Walking Gde)
Pembrokeshire Coast Path (British Walking Guide)
Pennine Way (British Walking Guide)
Peru's Cordilleras Blanca & Huayhuash – Hiking/Biking
The Railway Anthology
The Ridgeway (British Walking Guide)
Siberian BAM Guide – rail, rivers & road
The Silk Roads – a route and planning guide
Sahara Overland – a route and planning guide
Scottish Highlands – The Hillwalking Guide
Sinai – the trekking guide
South Downs Way (British Walking Guide)
Thames Path (British Walking Guide)
Tour du Mont Blanc
Trans-Canada Rail Guide
Trans-Siberian Handbook
Travel Tales – Guy Arnold
Trekking in the Everest Region
The Walker's Anthology
The Walker's Haute Route – Mont Blanc to Matterhorn
West Highland Way (British Walking Guide)

For more information about Trailblazer and our
expanding range of guides, for guidebook updates or
for credit card mail order sales visit our website:

www.trailblazer-guides.com

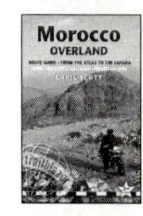